THE

RULES

OF

PARENTING

A personal code for bringing up
happy, confident children

RICHARD TEMPLAR

PEARSON

Harlow, England • London • New York • Boston • San Francisco • Toronto • Sydney
Auckland • Singapore • Hong Kong • Tokyo • Seoul • Taipei • New Delhi
Cape Town • São Paulo • Mexico City • Madrid • Amsterdam • Munich • Paris • Milan

PEARSON EDUCATION LIMITED
Edinburgh Gate
Harlow CM20 2JE
Tel: +44 (0)1279 623623
Fax: +44 (0)1279 431059
Website: www.pearson.com/uk

First published 2008 (print)
Second edition published 2013 (print and electronic)
This edition published 2015 (print and electronic)

© Richard Templar 2008 (print)
© Richard Templar 2013, 2015 (print and electronic)

ISBN: 978-1-292-08804-4 (print)
       978-1-292-08806-8 (PDF)
       978-1-292-08807-5 (ePub)
       978-1-292-08805-1 (eText)

British Library Cataloguing-in-Publication Data
A catalogue record for the print edition is available from the British Library

Library of Congress Cataloging-in-Publication Data
A catalog record for the print edition is available from the Library of Congress

10 9 8 7 6 5 4 3 2 1
19 18 17 16 15

Cover design by Nick Redeyoff

Print edition typeset in 10.5/12pt ITC Berkeley Oldstyle Std by 71
Print edition printed and bound in Great Britain by Clays Ltd, Bungay, Suffolk

NOTE THAT ANY PAGE CROSS REFERENCES REFER TO THE PRINT EDITION

THE

RULES

OF

PARENTING

PEARSON

At Pearson, we believe in learning – all kinds of learning for all kinds of people. Whether it's at home, in the classroom or in the workplace, learning is the key to improving our life chances.

That's why we're working with leading authors to bring you the latest thinking and best practices, so you can get better at the things that are important to you. You can learn on the page or on the move, and with content that's always crafted to help you understand quickly and apply what you've learned.

If you want to upgrade your personal skills or accelerate your career, become a more effective leader or more powerful communicator, discover new opportunities or simply find more inspiration, we can help you make progress in your work and life.

Pearson is the world's leading learning company. Our portfolio includes the Financial Times and our education business, Pearson International.

Every day our work helps learning flourish, and wherever learning flourishes, so do people.

To learn more, please visit us at **www.pearson.com/uk**

For Rich

'We are Earth's best that learnt her lesson here.
Life is our cry. We have kept the faith!'
(The Hill *by Rupert Brooke*)

Contents

Everyday Rules 54

Introduction

Nothing can prepare you for being a parent. It tests your stamina, your nerves, your emotions and at times even your sanity. You start out fretting over how to change a nappy or bath the baby without drowning it, and before long you discover that that's the least of your challenges. And just when you think you've got one phase of childhood cracked, they grow a bit older and it's a whole new scenario. Toddling, school, boyfriends or girlfriends, driving lessons – it never stops. Luckily the rewards are huge – the fun, the hugs and the closeness. Even the thanks eventually, if you're very lucky. And of course the pleasure of seeing them grow into the kind of person you can be proud of.

Along the way there's sure to be plenty of frustration, angst, bewilderment and soul searching as you look for the right things to say and do that will set your child on the road to growing up into a happy, well-balanced adult. And that's what this book is about.

The path you're now treading is well worn – millions of people have been parents before you, and by trial and error some of them have worked a few things out that might just be useful to you now. I've been through the parenting cycle twice. I've had two families spread over a total of nearly 30 years. That means I've had the chance to make most of the classic mistakes several times. But it also means that, through my friends and my children's friends, I've had the chance to watch and observe other families in action and see how other parents behave. It's an endlessly fascinating study.

Some parents seem to know instinctively how to handle every situation. Others get some bits wrong, but have brilliant ways of dealing with certain issues. If you study other parents long enough, as I have, you begin to spot patterns – tactics, techniques and principles of behaviour that get the best out of children, and that can be adapted whatever the personality of the child. It's those attitudes and principles that have been distilled into the *Rules of Parenting*, to guide you through the tough times, help you bring your child up to be all they can be, and improve the relationship between you for life.

The *Rules of Parenting* aren't intended to be a revelation – they are a reminder. Many are common sense, but it's easy to lose sight of them when you are dealing with a 2-year-old having a tantrum or a teenager who thinks the world and everything in it exists solely for their benefit. So even the seemingly obvious ones are worth putting in front of you again. After all, it's an important job to get right.

Over one hundred Rules might seem like a lot at first glance. But then, 18 years is a pretty long contract for a job. More than 18 if you have more than one child.* You've got to get your kids through weaning, nappies, toddling, learning to talk, the three Rs, school, friends, sex and drugs and rock-'n'-roll. Actually, 109 Rules isn't much at all.

It seems pretty clear to me how you can tell a good parent. You just have to look at their children. Some kids go through bad patches for a while for all sorts of reasons, many of which you really can't pin on the parents, but I've found that once they leave home, you can see what kind of a job their parents did. And I figure the parents whose kids are able to look after themselves, to enjoy life and to make those around them happy, to be caring and kind, and to stand up for what they believe in – those parents are the ones who are getting it right. And over the years I've seen what kind of parenting produces those kinds of adults 18 years on.

When you think about the huge responsibility you have as a parent, it can stop you in your tracks and take your breath away.

---

* Yes, I know, not if they're twins. Thank you.

What you do and say over the years will have a huge influence on whether your child grows up to be screwed up or well balanced. The good news is that by thinking about it all now, as you will if you read through this book, you'll automatically begin to correct many of your little foibles or bad habits as well as introducing new more helpful ones (helpful for you and your offspring).

There's more good news. There are lots of wrong ways to bring up your kids, but there are lots of right ones too. What you'll find in this book are principles to follow, which you can adapt to suit you and your children. There's no list of instructions you have to follow to the letter if you don't want your child to end up a loser. I've seen parents find all kinds of original, creative and unusual ways of interpreting these Rules successfully. It's about following the spirit, not the letter. For example, I've known great parents who home educated their kids, excellent parents whose children went to the local comprehensive, and equally successful parents whose kids boarded at public school. If you've got the right attitude, the rest will follow on.

I can personally vouch for the fact that it's impossible to get all the Rules spot on every day for 18 years. But then, I also know that all the best parents I've watched have messed up here and there. Just not too badly, and not too often, and they've always known when they've gone wrong. That seems to be very important: recognize where you've gone wrong and try harder to remember next time. That's as much as anyone can ask. And, from the kids I've watched grow up, that's good enough.

I can also tell you (and you may be relieved to hear this) that none of the Rules requires you to brush your child's hair religiously, or make sure they have clean socks every day. I'm sure that's all very nice, but I've also seen parents bring up their kids brilliantly with messy hair and no socks at all.

These Rules are about the important stuff. Things to do with your child's attitudes and values and self-image, not to do with their socks. They are Rules which will help you and your child to enjoy each other, enjoy life, and treat other people with respect. They are broad principles which apply equally in traditional nuclear families and in more modern formats such as single-parent or step-families.

I'm not claiming that there are exactly 109 Rules you have to follow and there will never be any more. Far from it. These are the Rules that I have observed as being the most important, but I'm always interested to hear from you and would love to collect more Rules of parenting if you have any up your sleeve. You're welcome to post your very own Rules on my Facebook page at www.facebook.com/richardtemplar

Richard Templar

RULES FOR STAYING SANE

This book is divided into 11 sections, and I'm starting with Rules for staying sane. After all, if you can't manage that, the other 108 Rules are going to be rather pointless.

If you're a very new parent – or about to become a parent for the first time – I don't want to alarm you by giving the impression that keeping madness at bay is the main occupation for parents, and that you'll be spending the next 18 years balancing on the edge of insanity. Not at all. It will only be moments of insanity you need to watch out for. There will be times when the moments are blissfully few and far between. But trust me when I say we all have these moments. Frankly, there are moments that challenge even the best Rules parents of them all.

The point here is that you'll enjoy the thing a whole lot more if you stay sane. Your sanity isn't only important because you are important, but also because your children need sane parents. And there are just a few Rules that you'll find, once you get the hang of them, help you keep your head when all about you are bawling theirs off.

Relax

So who are the best parents you know? The ones who have a seemingly instinctive ability to say and do the things that will result in happy, confident, well-balanced children? Have you ever wondered what makes them so good at it? Now think about the ones you privately don't think are much cop. Why not?

All the best parents I know have one key thing in common. They're relaxed about it. And all the worst ones are hung up on something. Maybe they're not stressed out about how good they are as parents (perhaps they should be) but they're hung up about something that affects their ability to be a really good parent.

I know a couple of parents who are neurotically clean and tidy. Their children have to take their shoes off at the door or the whole world falls apart. Even if the shoes are clean. They get really uptight if their children leave anything out of place or make any kind of a mess (even if it gets cleared up later). It makes it impossible for the kids just to relax and enjoy them-selves, in case they get grass stains on their trousers, or knock over the ketchup bottle.

I have another friend who is so obsessively competitive that his children are under huge pressure to win every friendly game they ever play. And one who frets excessively every time her child grazes his knees. I bet you can think of plenty of similar examples among people you know.

The really good parents I've encountered, on the other hand, expect their children to be noisy, messy, bouncy, squabbly, whingy and covered in mud. They take it all in their stride. They know they've got 18 years to turn these small creatures into respectable grown-ups, and they pace themselves. No rush to get them acting like adults – they'll get there in good time.

Between you and me, this Rule gets easier with time, though some people still never master it the way true Rules parents do. It's much harder to relax fully with your first baby than with your last teenager to leave home. With babies, you need to focus on the essentials – a healthy baby that isn't too hungry or too uncomfortable – and don't sweat the rest of it. It doesn't matter if their poppers are done up wrong, or you didn't find time to bath them today, or you've gone away for the weekend without anything for them to sleep in (yes, I have a friend who has done this, and no, she didn't sweat it, being a Rules parent).

Much better altogether if you can get to the end of each day, put your feet up with a glass of wine or a G&T,* and say cheerfully to each other, 'What the hell . . . they're all still alive so we must have got something right'.

> # REALLY GOOD PARENTS EXPECT THEIR CHILDREN TO BE NOISY, MESSY, BOUNCY, SQUABBLY, WHINGY AND COVERED IN MUD

---

* No, I'm not encouraging parents to use alcohol to get them through. Just relax!

No one is perfect

Have you ever thought what it would be like to have perfect parents? Well, think about it now. Imagine your parents had been faultless when you were growing up (I'm betting they weren't).* Suppose they were textbook parents – that your mother was *always right*. Sound like fun? Of course not.

Look, kids need something to kick against when they're growing up. They need someone to blame, and I'm afraid that's your job. So you might as well give them something to blame you for.

So what's it going to be? Nothing cruel or abusive of course – you need to pick something that's not unreasonable and shows a bit of human frailty. Maybe you've got a fuse that's just a little bit shorter than it should be? Perhaps you tend to put a bit too much pressure on them? Could it be that you're slightly neurotic about keeping everything tidy and ordered? Or tell you what, better still, why bother to choose? Just go with your own natural imperfections, and then you don't have to make an effort. Chances are you have a character flaw or two that will come in handy here.

Of course this doesn't mean that you're off the hook, that you shouldn't try to improve your parenting skills. Apart from anything else, that would make the rest of this book redundant. It just means that you shouldn't give yourself too hard a time when you fall a bit short of the standards you set yourself. After all, what kind of an example would it be to your kids if you were unable ever to fail, even a little bit? I wouldn't fancy having to live up to parents like that, and I don't suppose your children would either.

Your children are going to blame you for something, because that's how it works. If you were perfect, they'd have every reason to

---

* Please don't write in to accuse me of insulting your mother. I'm just making a point.

blame you for that. You can't win. You can only hope that eventually, especially if they become parents themselves, they'll come to see that actually they should be grateful to you for not being perfect.

> **YOUR CHILDREN ARE GOING TO BLAME YOU FOR SOMETHING, BECAUSE THAT'S HOW IT WORKS**

Be content

Contented parents make for contented kids. I certainly found out when I was growing up that stressed parents *don't* make their kids relaxed and at ease. So it stands to reason that you need to make sure you're as happy and relaxed as you can be.

This isn't some guilt trip to make you feel bad every time you're grumpy or unhappy. Not at all. Quite the reverse, in fact. Our kids need to learn to read people's emotions and recognize that everyone has their off moments. We all have bad days and tough experiences that affect our moods, but there are also things we can control. Aspects of our lives where we can make choices that leave us happier than the alternative. And the very fact that a certain choice makes us less stressed is in itself a good reason to make it. I'm not talking here about day-to-day mood swings, but about making big decisions that will reduce your stress levels in the long term.

So if breastfeeding your baby makes you feel really rotten and though you've really stuck at it, it's still making your stress levels rocket, you're probably doing your child a favour by choosing to bottle feed them, whatever anyone else may tell you. Sure, the milk itself may be less perfect, and in an ideal world breastfeeding is better, but this isn't an ideal world and that's only one aspect of the equation. Sometimes bottle feeding really is the formula for a happy baby (sorry, couldn't resist that one).

Here's another example. Some families – entirely understandably in my view – find holidays abroad deeply stressful. Yes, they're supposed to be relaxing, and you feel you 'ought' to enjoy them, but actually they never seem to turn out to be all that pleasurable. I once saw it described as 'hard work in a different place'. The effort of getting everything sorted, buying and transporting all the stuff you might need as you don't know what's at the other end, maybe having jabs, travelling long distances with fidgety kids, and then finding at the other end that the kids struggle to cope with a dramatically different temperature and are cranky, and won't eat anything that's available . . . Not exactly the recipe for a calm, happy family able to fully enjoy their time together. So why not give yourself a break? Find somewhere in your own country to holiday. It may not be as exotic, but if it means you can relax more and enjoy the holiday, surely it's better for everyone? Once the kids are older you can think about taking holidays overseas again.

In the end your mood is as important as your childrearing strategy and how you live as a family, if not more so. So don't let anyone guilt-trip you about the way you do it. If it makes you more relaxed and less stressed, it's probably the right thing to do – whatever it is.

> YOUR MOOD IS AS
> IMPORTANT AS YOUR
> CHILDREARING STRATEGY

RULE 4

Know what you're good at

When my oldest children were small, I was always jealous of those other dads who spent hours kicking a football around with their children. I felt slightly guilty that I couldn't do it for more than a few half-hearted minutes. It just wasn't me.

Then there was the friend who built a fabulous treehouse for his kids in their back garden ('Dad, why can't we have a treehouse like theirs?'). And the mother who created complex and intriguing treasure hunts for every party. And the one who took her daughter to the same ballet class as mine every week, but managed to look as if she was actually enjoying it, and . . . I could go on.

You're probably ahead of me here. I was focusing on what they could do that I couldn't, but actually I could do lots of things *they* couldn't – all things I took for granted, but just as valuable.

For example, I love reading aloud to children. And being a fairly outgoing kind of a chap (alright, verging on the exhibitionist), I really relished spending hours reading long stories, doing all the voices and accents and characterisations and sound effects and dramatic whispers and all the rest of it. But it seemed so natural that it was years before I realized that it was just as valuable a skill as treehouse-building or playing football.

On those increasingly rare occasions when I've kicked a football around with the kids, it's been perfectly clear that I'm only really doing it because I feel I should. That's not a bad reason, and it's still worth doing, but I'll never be like my friend whose enthusiasm for the game shone through and inspired his children. Then again, he probably can't read a story aloud like I can. Or cook such a mean spaghetti bolognese.

The thing is, Rules parents know what they're good at. We don't give up on everything else, but we play to our strengths. If we're rubbish at football, we read more stories; we provide lots of delicious home baking; we're endlessly patient with them learning the piano; we teach them how to fix cars; we share their enthusiasm for *Star Wars* or motorbikes or *My Little Pony* (yes, I know, you'd have to work really hard at that one).

It's important to know what you're good at, and to have confidence in your own strengths. That way, you can watch other parents doing things that you never could, without feeling inadequate. After all, you and I both know that those other parents can't do everything either. Whenever you feel a hint of jealousy rising, just stop and remind yourself of what you're great at.

> # RULES PARENTS DON'T GIVE UP ON EVERYTHING ELSE, BUT WE PLAY TO OUR STRENGTHS

Almost any rule can be broken occasionally

We all know that there are rules and systems and procedures and policies that must be followed if you're a parent. You know the sort of thing: don't feed them junk food, don't let them stay up too late, don't let their eyes turn square in front of the TV, don't allow them to swear until they're old enough (before you ask, see Rule 83).

What we Rules parents also understand is that there are very few rules that you can't break with a good enough reason. OK, you're supposed to feed them good healthy food and the recommended '5 a day', but when you get home tired after a long day, it's not the end of the world to give them fishfingers for once.

It's just a matter of thinking through what's the worst that can happen if you break this rule. Sure, if you break the rule about doing your seat belt up in the car the worst is pretty dire, so best keep to that one. But if you skip the bedtime bath because you're all exhausted – well, come on, how bad can that be?

Remember, this section is about Rules for staying sane. And the point of this Rule is to recognize that it's more important for your children to have a sane, relaxed parent than it is never to eat a fishfinger. Some parents make life far too difficult for themselves by thinking that it's essential to stick to every rule at all times. They beat themselves up over some tiny thing.

We once took two of our children for a day out that started with a steam train ride. The youngest was only a few weeks old, and the other was 2. It was only when we got out of the car at the station that we realized that the 2-year-old had no shoes. Now, of course, there's an unwritten rule that you don't take your children out for the day on steam trains without any shoes. We had two choices: abandon the train ride, or go ahead in bare feet. The 2-year-old, of course, favoured option two and headed for the train determined to vote with his feet.

That left us with two further choices: beat ourselves up over it, or go with the flow. Well, as you and I know, the only sensible Rules choice is to let it go. Either we – and our 2-year-old – enjoy a fun barefoot day out, or we get stressed over something we can't change and ruin his day as well as our own. It was one of those times when a rule has to be broken (but, of course, not the best day to break the 'have a bath before bedtime' rule as well).

So the moral of the story is, if you insist that every rule has to be followed every time, you're breaking Rule 5. Ha!

AS YOU AND I KNOW, THE

ONLY SENSIBLE RULES

CHOICE IS TO LET IT GO

RULE 6

Don't try to do everything

So what do you want your child to be when they grow up? Champion jockey? Ballerina? Scientist? Professional footballer? Concert violinist? Actor? Hard to be sure when they're young, so maybe you should keep all their options open by making sure they have extra tuition in everything they show any interest in. That way they can't complain later that it's your fault they failed because you didn't start them young enough.

It does make for a bit of a busy schedule of course. Football on Monday, drama on Tuesday, clarinet on Wednesday – and swimming after that. Thursday is ballet and Friday they do gym. And riding at the weekend. And that's just one child. It gets really fun if you have two or three.

Whoa. Hold on there. We're missing something. What about playing happily in the garden? What about learning to find their own entertainment? Where in the weekly schedule do they manage to browse through a comic, or even just mooch about staring at the clouds and thinking of nothing in particular? These are all vital parts of growing up too.

You know all those kids whose life is one long round of lessons and practice and extra tuition? Have you ever seen what happens when you ask them to fend for themselves for a few days? Suppose they go on holiday to some beautiful, peaceful place – the mountains, or the coast, or rolling countryside. Clueless, that's what. They've no idea how to enjoy themselves – they've never had time to learn. That's going to make adulthood really tough for them. They can't ever relax because no one's ever taught them how to.

Don't panic, I'm not suggesting you ban your children from all extra-curricular activities. That would just be silly. But I am suggesting you limit them to, say, two activities a week. And let them choose which two. No making them learn the violin just because you learnt it as a child and loved it. Or because you never learnt it and wished you had. If they want to take up something else, they'll have to drop one of their current activities to make room. (Yes, they're allowed to drop ballet if they hate it, even if the teacher did say she thought they had real talent.)

Remember those chilled, relaxed parents in Rule 1? How many of the best parents you know take their children to different activities almost every day of the week? None of them. They let them learn a couple of activities they're really interested in, and the rest of the time their kids amuse themselves dressing up, doing jigsaws, getting muddy, making things out of empty cereal packets, looking for bugs in the garden, lining up all their toy dinosaurs, reading books that are too young for them, and doing all those other things that kids are supposed to do because it's good for them, and it keeps them off your back.

> YES, THEY'RE ALLOWED
> TO DROP BALLET IF THEY
> HATE IT, EVEN IF THE TEACHER
> DID SAY SHE THOUGHT THEY
> HAD REAL TALENT

You don't have to follow every piece of advice you get (including this one)

What was it your mother told you? You have to wind the baby every ten minutes during a feed. Oh, and your mother-in-law said it's much better to buy clothes that don't go on over their head. And of course your best friend advised against getting a Moses basket. Although your brother-in-law said theirs was a lifesaver . . . aaargh!

And that's just the beginning. The amount of advice you get hit with when you have a new baby is terrifying. And 18 years later it still won't have stopped: 'Oh you don't want them to go to university. Waste of time – tell them to get a job instead.' Or, 'You want to get them out of the house now they're 18 or they'll still be there when they're 30'. Or, 'Don't buy them a car. Make them save up for it themselves. That's what we did'.

There's only really one person you absolutely must listen to: yourself. And if you're in this with a partner, it's probably wise to take their view into account as well. But leave it at that; otherwise you'll go mad. And you're supposed to be staying sane, if you remember.

I'm not saying you shouldn't listen to what they have to say if you want to. You might even pick up a useful tip or two. But even if they're right, you still don't have to do what they say. Just because a particular approach, ploy, piece of equipment, system, technique or whatever works for someone else, it doesn't mean it will work for you. All children are different and all parents are different, so it's hardly likely that their advice will work for you.

My neighbour once asked my opinion on whether she should try and get her new baby into a routine of feeds and naps. There was no point asking me – we were chalk and cheese. She was very orderly and precise and organized and would get really stressed if everything wasn't exactly so. I, on the other hand, am much more laid back and was happy for my kids to sleep when they were tired and eat when they were hungry.

Rules parents have the confidence to reject advice that just doesn't sound right for them. So by all means listen, and then run it through your own personal filter system. If that tip doesn't feel right, it probably isn't. Just smile politely and say, 'Thank you. I'll bear that in mind'.

> ## JUST BECAUSE A PARTICULAR APPROACH WORKS FOR SOMEONE ELSE, IT DOESN'T MEAN IT WILL WORK FOR YOU

RULE 8

It's normal to want to escape

Hey, let's talk taboos. Death, drugs, Morris dancing . . . or how about one of the biggest of all: admitting that there are times you wish your kids would just clear off?

Of course it's strictly forbidden ever to admit that your little darlings can be little toerags. You can joke about it self-deprecatingly, but you can't actually let on seriously that there are times you just want to escape from them. How could you? Your job is to love them and, if you love them, it follows that you love everything about them. You're supposed to smile indulgently when you're expected to read the same tedious story every night for three months, gaze adoringly as they shriek gratingly while racing around wildly, and laugh with them as they repeat the same unfunny joke for the twenty-fifth time – wrongly.

Funny thing is, it's considered fine to be irritated by other people's children (not that you're supposed to say so to their face). So we all know kids can get on our nerves. Which is why it follows that your own kids can drive you mad at times. And that's OK.

In fact, they're very good at it. They start pretty much as soon as they're born. That newborn cry is meant to bore into your brain until you do something about it. And boy, does it work. From then on in they get on your nerves routinely. Sometimes it's not even their fault. Actually, the most guilt-ridden thing of all is when you know it's not their fault. But when they've kept you up for three nights in a row teething, it's hard to be sympathetic. You know you should, but actually you just want them to *shut up* and let you sleep. It's only a tooth, after all.

Well, I have news for you. Every parent feels the same now and again. In fact there'll be phases when you feel that way 50 times a day, in between the phases where it's only once or twice a week.

Just accept that it's natural, and any parent who won't admit to that is lying. You can't stop your child getting on your nerves, but you don't have to do the guilt stuff as well.

The thing is, you have to remember that it cuts both ways. Remember being a child yourself? No matter how much they drive you mad, chances are high that you're getting on *their* nerves at least as much. So you're quits.

IT'S CONSIDERED FINE TO BE IRRITATED BY OTHER PEOPLE'S CHILDREN. SO WE ALL KNOW KIDS CAN GET ON OUR NERVES

RULE 9

You're allowed to hide from your kids

If Rule 8 says that your kids are allowed to drive you mad, it follows that you have to be allowed to do something about it. Personally, I'm in favour of running away and hiding. No, seriously, I've been known to nip into the nearest cupboard and hold my breath until they've left the room.

You know the feeling. You can hear them getting closer and closer, saying, 'I'm telling on you!' 'No, I'm telling on *you!*' You just know that you're the one they're planning to tell, and you have no idea who did what to whom or whether it was justified. What is the Rules parent supposed to do? Well, the answer is obvious to me: you hide. And do you know what? When they can't find you, they almost always sort it out for themselves.

Lots of parenting books will tell you about using 'time out' when your kids misbehave. You know, you send them to their room, or to the 'naughty step' (don't get me started on that one),* until they have calmed down. It can work very well, but why should the kids get all the fun? You have to be allowed 'time out' too. When you need to calm down, you can award it to yourself. That means getting away from the kids any way you can – including hiding.

I have a friend who told me – many years ago, shortly before my first child was born – that there were times having a baby left her so exhausted and frustrated she just wanted to lash out. The prospect of this rather worried me, and I asked her what she did about it. She told me that there was only one solution. Put the baby down in the middle of the floor where it could come to no

---

* It always seems unfair to single out one particular step. How can one step be so much more badly behaved than all the other steps?

harm, and then go far enough away that she couldn't hear it yell, until she had regained her composure.

Why is it that so many of us feel we shouldn't do that, even when we've reached breaking point? We feel we're failing in some way as parents, but actually we're taking the most logical solution there is. Well, Rules parents understand that we're all human, and we all need to run away and hide sometimes. That way we can do a far better job when we return refreshed.

I'VE BEEN KNOWN TO NIP INTO THE NEAREST CUPBOARD AND HOLD MY BREATH UNTIL THEY'VE LEFT THE ROOM

RULE 10

Parents are people too

When was the last time you had a meal out without the kids? Spent an evening with friends and didn't mention the children once? Got drunk? Spent half a day tinkering with an engine or pottering in the garden or however you used to while away happy hours before the children came along?

I hope it wasn't too long ago. If you let it, being a parent can take over your life. We Rules parents need to know when to switch off. Of course you're only ever on standby, not switched off at the wall, but you can have a lot of fun on standby.

Listen, this one is really important because – apart from anything else – if your kids are your entire life, that puts a huge amount of pressure on them. On some level they'll realize that your personal success is founded entirely on how well they perform, and how they turn out. That's a pretty heavy burden to dump on a child.

This Rule is much harder to follow in the early months – in fact I'll let you off the first three months – but you need to set the pattern as early as you can. Your children need you to have a life apart from them; otherwise it's extremely hard for them to have their own lives as they grow older. And anyway, if you lock yourself away and construct your whole life around feeding times and naps, you'll open the door in a few years' time and find you have no friends. And how will that help?

I've noticed over the years that the Rules parents I most admire always have interests that don't have anything to do with being a parent. Maybe they have careers they're passionate about, or they holiday on their own once a year, or they make sure they never miss tennis on a Thursday, or go boating every Saturday, or the cup final, or April in Paris, or whatever it is that keeps them sane.

Hey, I know it's tough and time is at a premium. Of course you'll do less clubbing and take fewer drugs* than you did before the kids came along. But you need to make sure that you hang on to at least part of the things that you enjoy most. Otherwise, when the kids finally leave home after 18 years, you won't know what to do with yourself.

> THE RULES PARENTS I MOST ADMIRE ALWAYS HAVE INTERESTS THAT DON'T HAVE ANYTHING TO DO WITH BEING A PARENT

---

* Only joking – don't write in.

RULE 11

Don't ignore your relationship with your partner

This Rule is pretty obvious. The tough bit is actually doing it. Lots of parents pay it lip-service, but far fewer really make sure it happens. But you and I know that it really is one of the most vital Rules of the lot, if you don't want to end up doing this whole parenting lark on your own.

You loved this person enough to have babies with them. That's serious stuff. They should still be the most important person in your life. They may take up less time and possibly demand less attention than your children, but they should still be the object of your love. Having children changes your relationship more than you might have thought possible, but 20 years on it'll be you and your partner again just like it was at the start. And if they're not the most important thing in your life, you're going to be screwed when the kids leave home. And so are the kids – leaving home is tough enough without feeling you're tearing your parents' world apart into the bargain. They need to know that you love each other best of all. That frees them up to get on with their lives and, eventually, find a partner they can love even more than they love you.

Part of the solution is logistical. Aim to go out on your own together once a week. If you can't afford a babysitter, find some other parents and take it in turns to mind each other's kids. Then just go for a walk or have fish & chips in the park. Something. Anything. Just make sure you perpetuate that 'just the two of us' life you had before.

If that's tricky (if you have more than one child you'll know what I mean . . . whoosh, where did all those offers of babysitting go?), then go out for the walk with the little ones but talk about each other, instead of rabbiting on about what the baby did yesterday.

And then there's sex. Yes, of course, we all know it's hard to make time when you're exhausted, busy with the baby, run down, feeling unsexy, and the baby is watching from the cot next to your bed. And asking you to swing from the chandeliers may be too much. But you can still set aside an evening for a special meal or a romantic film, followed by a sexy massage. I know you've heard it all before, but it still works. If you make the effort, and you really give each other love and attention, you'll be glad you did. Concentrate on quality more than quantity (within reason) for a little while if that helps. And once the kids get a bit older, well, maybe the chandelier will even be back on the menu.

> ## YOU LOVED THIS PERSON ENOUGH TO HAVE BABIES WITH THEM. THAT'S SERIOUS STUFF

ATTITUDE
RULES

A big part of being a Rules parent is getting the attitude right. Once you've learnt to think the right way about your children and about what you're doing, most of the rest of it falls into place.

So this section is all about how to get the attitude that goes with being a Rules parent. Your attitude to your children and your attitude to the job of being a parent. You need to see your children in the best light in order to enjoy them as much as possible and give them the upbringing they need. If you see them as demons, or angels, or anything else negative or unrealistic, you're going to find the next few years pretty tough.

It's all about building the right relationship from the start so that your kids can grow and become gradually more independent, and you can get as much as they do out of it.

Love is not enough

How many times have you heard the cliché, 'The most important thing you can give your children is love'? Well, yes, obviously love is essential. I think we've all worked that one out. But if that was all you gave them, they would be missing out badly.

Hippy-style parents (I know about them – I was one once) often seem to imagine that children should be allowed to run wild and free with the wind in their hair and the earth beneath their feet, happy because they know you love them. You should never try to restrain them (you're controlling them) or limit their behaviour (you're putting metaphorical bars around them).

Excuse me a moment.

Ah, that's better. I've just been to throw up. Back again now.

I used to live in Glastonbury so I've watched my share of hippy children grow up like this. Once they reached adulthood they struggled to find their way in the real world, and struggled to have grown-up relationships with friends and workmates. Some of them struggled to gag down a normal meal having been fed entirely on sprouting chickpeas for 18 years. I even know a couple who moved abroad to escape from their parents.

Yes, yes, yes – you have to give your children love. But there are a few other things you have to give them too: discipline, self-discipline, values, the ability to form good relationships, a healthy lifestyle, a range of interests, a decent education, a broad mind, the ability to think for themselves, an understanding of the value of money, the skills to be assertive, the ability to learn – and the occasional haircut.

Hey, nobody said it was going to be easy. You took on a big job when you had kids, and it's going to be hard work for the rest of your life. No good thinking all you have to do is love them and you can tick the 'I'm a great parent' box. Letting them do what they want when they want is not good for them so you have to get involved and that means your blood, sweat and tears. But hey, look around you; plenty of parents are getting it right so it can't be that difficult – but you do have to recognize that you've got a big task ahead of you. Lucky, really, that you've got 18 years to get it all done.

> YOU TOOK ON A BIG JOB
> WHEN YOU HAD KIDS, AND
> IT'S GOING TO BE HARD
> WORK FOR THE REST OF
> YOUR LIFE

RULE 13

Every recipe needs different ingredients

Rule 12 says you have to do a lot more than just love them. So what you gonna do? Well, there's not just one simple answer to that, and some of it depends on your child's personality and on your circumstances. That's what this Rule is for.

You can't just follow a set of instructions and apply it to every child you have without thinking. Children don't work like that. I have friends who applied the same basic approach to bringing up their three children, and everything went smoothly. Then along came child number four, and he was completely different. He saw the world in a different way. He couldn't accept authority. He had trouble understanding people. He was delightful but seriously quirky. For example, he insisted on sleeping in his clothes every night on the grounds that it was pointless taking them off if he was just going to put them back on again as soon as he woke up.

My friends clashed with their son constantly because he didn't live up to their expectations of a well-behaved child the way the other three did. But they had the sense to sit down together and discuss what did and didn't work with him, and why, and to think through whether it was fair – or productive – to set him the same standards as the others. They adapted some of their rules and not others. It doesn't matter which – the point is that they really thought about what they were doing, and why.

And you know what? They started questioning and thinking about how they treated the older three as well, and they found the process helped those relationships get even better too.

The trick was to look at all the areas where there was conflict, or where they could see one of their children was upset or worried, and to question why and how they could help.

The thing is, if you don't think about what you're doing, you're pretty unlikely to get it right. After all, if you didn't think about the shopping before you started, you'd come back from the supermarket with an unhelpful assortment of things. If you didn't think about what you wanted from a holiday before you left, you'd have less chance of enjoying it. In the same way, if you don't think about how you bring your kids up, you may muddle through OK, but you won't be doing your best for them.

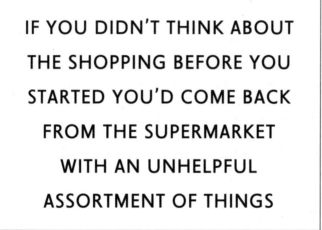

IF YOU DIDN'T THINK ABOUT
THE SHOPPING BEFORE YOU
STARTED YOU'D COME BACK
FROM THE SUPERMARKET
WITH AN UNHELPFUL
ASSORTMENT OF THINGS

Anything extreme is almost certainly wrong

I know parents who never let their kids watch any TV. Not many of them, mind you. And I know parents who feed their children an exclusively vegan diet. And parents who dress their children entirely in pink. I even know parents who make their children get up at 6.30 every morning, even in the holidays – which may be normal in some parts of the world, but certainly not here in the UK.

Aha! That's the crux of it, you see. None of these things may be wrong in themselves, but it just doesn't work to bring your children up in ways that are too much at odds with their peers. It messes with their sense of identity, and makes it even harder than it already is for them to feel comfortable in their own skin.

Personally, I think a world where no children ever watched any TV (didn't we have one of those once?) might be a very good thing. But in a world where all their friends watch TV, it's just not a viable restriction to inflict on your own children. Sure, you can impose more restrictions than many of their friends' parents do. But don't stop them altogether. Children want to fit in, and anything that makes them stand out as different will be tough for them to cope with.

When it comes to most aspects of bringing up kids – bedtimes, pocket money, TV, music practice, dress style, food and all the rest – there's generally a range of behaviour within your social group. If your attitude and house rules fall anywhere within that range, you're doing fine. But you want to think very carefully before you step outside the 'normal' range for where you live and who your kids hang out with. Move to one end of the range if you wish, by all means, but stay inside those invisible boundaries.

I used to know a child whose parents smacked her with a ruler whenever she misbehaved. They came from a different country, where such things were normal, but this poor girl didn't have any classmates or friends whose parents punished their children in this way. She didn't know what to think, and indeed she went through a long stage of being physically aggressive towards other children who didn't do as she wanted. Her parents' attitudes weren't being reinforced among her teachers or her peers, so she was just plain confused.

One of my children goes to a school where we have to supply a packed lunch every day. Lots of his friends have chocolates, crisps, biscuits, cakes in their lunchbox. I know perfectly well that if we put the same things in my son's lunch, that's all he'd eat. So we like to keep it healthy. But he does get plenty of borderline healthy foods, and the occasional treat, because it just isn't fair otherwise.*

It's all relative, that's what I'm saying. Most parenting attitudes aren't simply right or wrong. A few obvious things are wrong, but sometimes what's right in one time or place may be wrong in another. You have to trim your style to suit your child's world – and anything extreme is generally wrong simply because it's extreme, regardless of its rightness in other respects.

> CHILDREN WANT TO FIT
> IN, AND ANYTHING THAT
> MAKES THEM STAND OUT AS
> DIFFERENT WILL BE TOUGH
> FOR THEM

---

* Of course, what we should do is send him to a school where they feed them on nothing but gruel every day, but there doesn't seem to be one of those round these parts.

Look pleased to see them

Now here's something that really gets my goat. I can't count the number of parents I've seen do this. Their child comes in from school or an afternoon out, and as they walk through the door they're greeted with, 'Take those muddy shoes off!' Or, 'Homework, now! Before you do anything else'.

I have a friend who once came home from school in the middle of the day with a huge bump on her head, after a fall in the gym. This was in the days when you were allowed to go home on your own after something like that happened. Her mum was busy mopping the kitchen floor as my friend appeared in the doorway. The mum looked up with wrinkled brow and said, 'You can't come in. The floor's wet'.

How are these children supposed to know their parents love them? After all, their mum and dad greet the dog, the grandparents, their children's friends, even the postman* more warmly than that.

The alternative practised by some parents is just to ignore the children when they come in, as if they were part of the furniture. This is just as bad, since giving them no attention at all is arguably as bad as giving them negative attention (that's wibble-speak for shouting at them).

Everyone is generally rushed at breakfast time on school days. But it takes no time at all to be friendly, and frankly anything that makes the kids a little bit less grumpy while you're trying to

---

* No offence to postmen. In fact we have two postmen and they can be relied on to give me a friendly greeting to start the day. They're known as Worm (he always turns up early) and Grub, though not to their faces.

get their hair brushed or shovel some food down them has to be worthwhile, doesn't it?

How hard can it be to give them a smile, and maybe a hug (if they haven't reached the age where they won't let you)? It's only a small thing, but it makes a huge difference to your kids. They just want to know that you're happy to see them.

And if their shoes really are filthy and you've just cleaned the kitchen floor (one might ask why, when the kids were about to appear in muddy shoes), you can still use humour to stop them in their tracks and then give them hugs and kisses for co-operating.

> # HOW HARD CAN IT BE TO GIVE THEM A SMILE, AND MAYBE A HUG?

Treat your child with respect

I know a mother who is always issuing her children with instructions: 'Eat your lunch.' 'Get in the car.' 'Clean your teeth.' The other day I heard her complaining about how hard it is to get her children to say please and thank you. Now you and I know exactly what her problem is, but she can't see it.

It's frighteningly easy to do, though. Children are supposed to do what you say, whereas other adults don't have to. So you ask the grown-ups nicely, but you just tell the kids what to do. The problem is that the kids don't see it like that. They don't notice how you speak to everyone else (after all, kids never listen). They just speak to you in the way you speak to them.

If your children have any sense they'll take more notice of what you do than of anything you say. So not only can you not blame them for skimping on the niceties if you do, but actually they should be congratulated on following your example.

Your children deserve respect, of course, simply because they're human. But on top of that, you won't get respect back from them if you don't show it. You won't be undermining your authority. Your kids will soon learn that 'Clean your teeth please' or 'Would you lay the table?' might sound like a request but actually they don't have a choice. You'll just be teaching them manners in the best way possible – by demonstration.

It's not only manners that they need to learn by example. You should never break promises to them, never lie to them (Father Christmas doesn't count), and never swear in front of them if you don't want them to copy you. If you do these things, you are telling your kids loud and clear (if not in so many words) that they are less important than other people and they don't matter. Now we know that isn't true. It's important that your children know it too.

If you love your children more than anyone else (except your partner), then they deserve your respect more than anyone else, not less. That way, they'll learn to treat other people with respect too. There, that's the problem of 'What's the younger generation coming to?' sorted.

> # YOUR CHILDREN DESERVE RESPECT, OF COURSE, SIMPLY BECAUSE THEY'RE HUMAN

RULE 17

Enjoy their company

If you baulked slightly when you read this Rule, I understand. In fact, I'll be the first to admit that there are times this one can be tough. But then, there are times you're not in the mood for your favourite movie or music or chocolate.*

Don't panic. This Rule doesn't mean you always have to be in the right mood to hang out with your kids. All I'm saying is that when you get a chance to relax with them – at weekends, on holiday, reading a bedtime story – it's important to enjoy being with them.

Why wouldn't you? Well, because you're always thinking of what else you could be doing, or the long list of chores you need to be getting on with instead of listening to the entire plot of yesterday's episode of *The Simpsons* being explained – badly – in real time, or worrying that the vegetables are about to boil over in the kitchen, or mentally running through tomorrow's presentation for work.

Stop! You are already in the middle of the most important task on your to-do list – enjoying your child's company. Stop thinking about something else and really concentrate on them, on what they're doing and saying. Recognize that this is as important as getting their nappy changed or sorting out the supper or writing that presentation. So have a proper conversation with them. When your child tells you 'Guess what? I just killed 17 orcs!', don't just mumble, 'Wow'. Instead try, 'Does that mean you've used up all your arrows?'

The trick to enjoying their company is to focus on it as an end in itself. OK, so you don't actually enjoy dressing Barbie up in a succession of glam outfits, or discussing the finer points of every football team in the league, or listening to a blow-by-blow account of an imaginary battle between the powers of light and a battalion

---

* OK, not the chocolate.

of invading aliens. You don't have to. These things are just a means to an end. The end objective is to spend time with your child, learning about how they view the world and what amuses, upsets, hurts, entertains, fascinates, bores and intrigues them.

Once you learn to stop and enjoy, you'll find your pleasure in your child's company increases hugely, and you really start to learn from them. And once you get good at doing it when you have the time, you'll be able to forgive yourself much more easily for those occasions when you really can't face another half hour of *My Little Pony*.

THE TRICK TO ENJOYING THEIR COMPANY IS TO FOCUS ON IT AS AN END IN ITSELF

RULE 18

It's not about you – it's about them

Let's be clear about something. Having kids isn't compulsory. You don't have to do it. But if you do decide you're going to go for it, you have to be prepared to put the kids first. No, that doesn't mean giving them everything they want – often the reverse is the case. But it does mean making decisions based on what's good for them, not what's good for you.

Do you want some for instances? OK then. I've known parents have their child sleep in their bed with them at 6 or 7 years old – not because it's what the child needs, but because the parent doesn't want to stop. It really is lovely having your child snuggle up next to you, but it doesn't help them to become independent, manage their own sleep patterns, overcome any anxiety about the dark and so on. And if it's not what all their friends are doing . . . well, I'd refer you back to Rule 14.

Here's another. A friend told me recently that her daughter really likes the look of a degree course at a uni a couple of hundred miles away. My friend said she was trying to put her daughter off, and persuade her to do a different course that runs at our local uni so she could live at home. I said I was sure her daughter would cope fine with being away at uni, to which my friend replied that she knew that, but that *she* wasn't ready to let go of her daughter yet.

What's best for your child is often best for you, too. But sometimes it isn't. Often we make excuses to justify ourselves (fair play to my friend, who at least admitted why she wanted to influence her child's choice of university). Parents will tell you that their child wakes in the night, for example, so it's easier to sleep in the same bed. We tell ourselves that our child isn't old enough to do this or that, or they're more anxious than most, or it's healthier this way, or it's impractical to let them do such and such.

But deep down, we know perfectly well what we're doing. We just aren't admitting it, even to ourselves. Because if we did, we'd have to switch to doing what suits our children instead. Sometimes it's very tough, but once we've made the choice to do the whole kids thing, we have to be honest with ourselves and put them first.

And actually, that's where the real joy in having kids comes. Putting other people first isn't a prison for ourselves – it's liberation. As long as we're focused on other people, we can't mope, pine for the past, be miserable, feel sorry for ourselves, harbour grudges – because all those things are about ourselves, and we're distracted when we think about other people. And who better than our own kids? Yes, it's warm and snug having your child all cosy in bed with you. But watching them grow into independent, capable adults trumps it every time.

> # DEEP DOWN, WE KNOW PERFECTLY WELL WHAT WE'RE DOING

Being tidy isn't as important as you think

When I first met my wife (at which point she wasn't my wife, obviously) I can remember being somewhat intimidated by her house. I have this memory of tables with almost nothing on them, clear work surfaces, vast open tracts of flooring with not a speck on them. You could pick up any object in my wife's house and ask her where it lived, and she could tell you. Yes, everything – and I mean everything – actually had a place where it was supposed to go.

This was a pretty new concept to me, I can tell you. I always belonged to the drop-it-on-the-floor-and-don't-give-it-a-second-thought school of domestic organization. I must confess that, when we decided to have children, I privately worried about how my wife would cope. I knew that her style of housekeeping wasn't compatible with the kind of relaxed, easy-going children we both wanted.*

In the event she adapted admirably, as many parents do. But not all manage it. Some persist, like Canute,** in trying to hold back the tide of mud, grime, mess, dust, books, toys, clutter and disorganization that come as standard issue with children. And that new category of objects that you can't ever put away because you have absolutely no idea what they are, so there's no hope of working out where they belong.

---

* I should say in my wife's defence, in case she sounds neurotically retentive, that despite being obsessively tidy, she never ironed anything, and her vacuum cleaner was only a distant acquaintance.

** Please don't bother explaining to me that this isn't what Canute was trying to do. I know he was only trying to prove a point. And I'm just trying to make one.

There are only two options here. Option one is to drive yourself increasingly round the bend neurotically trying to do the impossible and keep the house tidy, while turning your children into tense and stilted pseudo-adults who aren't allowed to behave naturally and have never worn shoes indoors. Option two is to give in, chill, relax, let up, allow your kids to be kids, and have a happy household with easy-going, laid-back kids despite the occasional muddy floor or messy room. I think we both know which is the Rules way.

I'm not saying that children should never tidy up after themselves. But let them enjoy themselves first and then clear up afterwards. It doesn't matter if the kitchen table is covered in finger paints, or their trousers are covered in mud. It all washes off. It *does* matter if they're not allowed to relax and have fun.

> # I'M NOT SAYING THAT CHILDREN SHOULD NEVER TIDY UP AFTER THEMSELVES. BUT LET THEM ENJOY THEMSELVES FIRST

RULE 20

Good parenting is calculated risk taking

When I was a teenager, my younger brother – aged about 8 – decided to climb a tall tree in the garden. He had reached approximately the height of the roof of the house when the branch he was standing on snapped. He grabbed onto the branch above with both hands and was left swinging about 25 ft above the ground (if you think only in metric, that's a long way). Not surprisingly, he yelled extremely loudly.

My mother came out to the garden to see what the trouble was. Her stomach must have lurched when she saw him so high up and so precarious, but she didn't show it. She simply talked him down reassuringly: 'It's OK, there's a small stump about three inches from your left foot. That's it. Now move your right hand down to the lower branch . . . ' and so on, until he was back on the ground.

You might have thought that my mother would ban tree-climbing after that, at least for a few years, but she didn't. She understood that my brother had learnt a useful lesson – which he had.

So what's my point? Well, children have to be allowed to learn their own lessons, make their own mistakes, find out the hard way. If they never take risks, they never learn. People who don't make mistakes don't make anything. And that means that *you* have to take risks. As a Rules parent you have to allow them to climb trees, let them take on more subjects at GCSE than you think they can handle, say yes to their first backpacking holiday.

You're the one who has to calculate the risk, of course. There are times when the stakes are too high and you will say no. But you can't always operate on a worst-case scenario principle. If you do that you'll say no to everything just because it's not guaranteed safe. And then your children will learn nothing, and will be ill-equipped to make their own decisions once they leave home. In which case you won't have done your job properly.

So expect to take risks. And of course, if you take risks, sometimes things will go wrong. Your child may end up with a fractured wrist or a poor exam result. But hey, things could be worse and they learn as much as you do from it. The alternative is no risks at all, which will do them far more harm in the long term.

> # YOU CAN'T ALWAYS OPERATE ON A WORST-CASE SCENARIO PRINCIPLE

RULE 21

Keep your worries to yourself

If your children are ever going to take risks, you're bound to worry. It goes with the territory. You'll worry when they climb trees, you'll worry when they learn to drive, you'll worry when they go off on holiday without you. In fact, even if you never take any risks, you'll still worry. You'll worry when they are out of your sight for the first time, you'll worry when they start school, you'll worry when they go for their first sleepover, you'll worry when their cheeks are flushed and their temperature won't come down, you'll worry when they have exams.

What you have to remember is that you're not the only one. Your kids worry about all these things too. Your little one may be terrified of starting school, your teenager may be incredibly nervous of going on holiday, but determined to make themselves do it.

Your job is to reassure them. Give them the confidence to go ahead. Make them feel that everything is fine. It's a bummer, eh? There you are, fretting away with your stomach full of butterflies, and you're supposed to smile placidly and make out it's all fine. Yep, that's the job, I'm afraid. It's tough, but somebody's gotta do it. And that somebody is you.

Your only consolation is that you can go and dump on another grown-up. Your partner maybe. Or, better still, your parents. Because even at your age, their job is still to tell you it's all going to be fine when you're worried sick.

And while we're on the subject, try and stop yourself saying 'Be careful' every time your child steps out of the door. Not only does it imply a lack of trust in your offspring, but a child who is told to 'be careful' when they carry something fragile is much more likely to drop it than if nothing is said. 'Be careful' can start to make a child think something is about to go wrong. A Rules parent thing to say would be 'Have a good time' or 'Enjoy yourself'. And you are a Rules parent now of course.

WHAT YOU HAVE TO REMEMBER IS THAT YOU'RE NOT THE ONLY ONE. YOUR KIDS WORRY TOO

RULE 22

See things from their point of view

All children have a huge chip on their shoulder. They're convinced that we take less notice of how they feel just because they're kids. They reckon we ignore them, we disregard their feelings, we don't care if our decisions upset them. And you know what? They're absolutely right.

We all do it. Not all the time, of course, but too much of the time. I know I do, and I've never met a parent who didn't. We tell ourselves (if we think about it at all) that we know what's best for them and they don't. Sometimes that's true, but not always.

Up to a point this is unavoidable. I mean, most kids will always want to go to bed later than is good for them. They'll usually want to live exclusively on ice cream and chocolate, and they'll want to play hooky from school for the next 11 years and go to the beach instead. OK, so we know this is a bad idea and we have to make them do it our way, but that still doesn't mean we can't see it from their point of view. Actually, I suspect that left to their own devices, most children would pretty soon start behaving a lot more sensibly than we give them credit for.

Look, children often view the world differently from us. Sometimes they view it the same way but we just don't think about their perspective. Either way, they get understandably stroppy when they think we're ignoring them. It's all part of Rule 16 – treat them with respect. So it's important to let them know that you can see their viewpoint. (If you can't see it, I'm sure they'll fill you in if you ask.)

The other day, I was just about to go out with the children and one of them was watching TV. So I told him to turn it off and get in the car. He flipped. I told him firmly that we had to pick someone up from the station, and that was more important than the TV. We had an argument about it. Both of us got heated and both of us hated it. I found myself wondering if there wasn't a better way.

Then I remembered Rule 22. So I asked my son to tell me what the problem was. He explained that it was his favourite programme and he'd missed it for the last two weeks. I sympathised and offered to record it for him. Problem solved. And actually, it was nothing to do with the programme itself, it was resolved because he felt I cared about his feelings. It would have helped if I'd remembered Rule 22 sooner of course – but I was busy following Rule 2 (no one is perfect). That's my excuse, anyway.

> ## CHILDREN GET UNDERSTANDABLY STROPPY WHEN THEY THINK WE'RE IGNORING THEM

Parenting is not a competitive sport

The other day I was talking to another parent about our children's eating habits. I commented on the fact that mine would snack on crisps and biscuits all the time if we kept them in the house (which is why we don't). 'Oh I'm lucky,' she said, 'mine would rather eat fruit and raw vegetables anyway'. Now, considering the way her two had recently tucked into the biscuits they'd been given as a treat, I doubt this is even true. But the point is that this was a classic competitive remark, intended purely to put me and my kids down, and thereby raise her and her kids up.

One of the classic competitive parenting events is potty training. I know parents who have started putting their babies on the pot at a few months old, simply so they can get ahead of their friends' children. Or itched to get their babies up on their feet and walking first. Or bragged about how well their child does in sport or music or exams. And the most underhand competitive parents of all are the ones who can't even boast openly but who dress it up in some other way – as in 'I'm lucky my kids would rather eat fruit than crisps', which you are not for a moment supposed to believe has anything to do with luck.

We Rules parents don't play the competitive parenting game. We are confident enough in our own skills – and relaxed enough about our imperfections – to go with the flow and lay off our kids. You see, not only do competitive parents rarely have many good friends (with kids), but they also have pressurised children, who feel compelled to perform well so their parents can continue to boast about them. These poor kids believe they can only get their parents' approval if they consistently outperform their friends. Eventually they grow up to be over-competitive too, which alienates potential friends, not to mention siblings. There are plenty of opportunities for kids to learn a bit of healthy competition without having to impose unhealthy competition at their expense.

See, the thing about competitive parents is that they're insecure, uptight and unsure of their skills as parents. That's why they have to put you down in order to bolster themselves up. So don't get annoyed. Just pity them. That will really rile them.

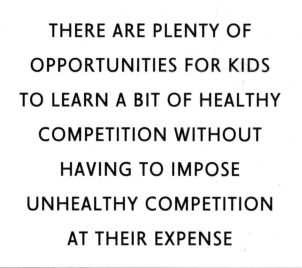

THERE ARE PLENTY OF OPPORTUNITIES FOR KIDS TO LEARN A BIT OF HEALTHY COMPETITION WITHOUT HAVING TO IMPOSE UNHEALTHY COMPETITION AT THEIR EXPENSE

Never emotionally blackmail them

Have you ever caught yourself saying any of the following (or variations on them)?

- 'After everything I've done for you, surely you can just do this for me?'

- 'You're making me sad.'

- 'It's not fair on me.'

Recognize any of those? If not, well done – go to the next page. If you have ever heard any of these words coming out of your mouth, you're certainly not alone. Nevertheless, these are all forms of emotional blackmail and thus a Bad Thing.

Emotional blackmail puts an underhand and insidious pressure on your children, and if you do it often your children will develop an unhelpful tendency to guilt, along with quite possibly a resentment towards you. What's more, you're indicating that your feelings are more important to you than theirs, and setting an example of putting oneself first, being self-pitying, and being emotionally manipulative.

Look, you got yourself into this parent thing. It's normal for kids to behave selfishly, and you're obviously going to be on the receiving end of that more often than anyone else. You have no right to take it out on them – it's not their problem if you're tired, overworked, stressed, feeling taken for granted.

I'm not suggesting that you should encourage your children to be selfish. But you need to find ways that don't entail emotionally blackmailing them. Point out the effect their actions have on other people, or just tell them straight. Instead of, 'Please don't ask me to play football with you when I'm so exhausted', you can simply say, 'I'm sorry, I'm too tired. I'll play with you tomorrow'.

There is simply no point in telling your children, 'I work my fingers to the bone for you – I cook for you, clean up after you, wash your clothes, take you to football practice, ferry you about in the car . . .'. I can tell you that all they hear is, 'Blah, blah, blah, football, blah, blah . . .'. So you're wasting your breath. It's quite true that someone needs to point all this out to them, but it isn't you. What you need is a partner or grandparent or big sister or someone to say, 'Don't drop your clothes on the floor like that. Why should your mum/dad pick up after you at your age? Don't you think they do enough for you already?' And you can do the same thing for your partner. The kids are far more likely to listen to that.

Another option is to offer to swap jobs with them for a day (preferably not a school day, or it gets tricky). You'll get up late and play or read most of the day, and they can do all your jobs. They'll probably decline your offer, but they'll have to think about what you do in order to make that decision.

So you see, there's no excuse for emotional blackmail because there are lots of better ways to teach your children not to be selfish – and ones which won't leave them emotionally scarred.

IT'S NORMAL FOR KIDS TO BEHAVE SELFISHLY, AND YOU'RE OBVIOUSLY GOING TO BE ON THE RECEIVING END OF THAT MORE OFTEN THAN ANYONE ELSE

EVERYDAY
RULES

Of course, it's all very well having virtuous broad principles to bring your children up by, but most of parenting is the day-to-day slog of getting them up and dressed, changing their nappies, or packing them off to school on time, persuading them to eat something halfway healthy, arguing about bedtime or debating whether you're going to pay for the new trainers they want.

So I'm guessing that what you really need now are some useful everyday Rules, to make all those daily interactions easier and more profitable, and to make having kids the fun you always hoped it would be, rather than the grind you sometimes fear it could turn into.

These are the Rules that ensure your kids grow into the intelligent, inquisitive, helpful adults you want them to be. At least on a good day.

Let them get on with it

I don't want to panic you, but by the time your child is 18 – if not before – they've got to be a fully functioning adult who is wise and capable enough to make their own decisions, make their own friends, make their own life, make their own bed, and make their own way across London on the tube system. Yep, you've got your work cut out.

If you're still spoon-feeding your child at 4 years old, and putting their homework books back in their school bag when they're 14, they're going to struggle when they have to look after themselves. So don't do anything for them if they can do it for themselves. And that not only means tidying up and doing their homework (personally, I find that by the age of about 8 my kids can do their own homework better than I could do it for them). It means getting them each to cook the family meal occasionally from the age of about 10, even if it is only beans on toast, and understanding how a washing machine works, and getting themselves out of bed for the Saturday job, and doing their own packing to go on holiday.

But even this isn't the most important thing. Oh no! There are two other skills in particular they need that you have to start teaching them as early as you can: the ability to manage their money and the ability to make their own decisions.

You see, if you control all their money from the outset, and just give them a bit of spending money, they learn nothing. Much better, as they get older, to make them responsible for a clothing allowance, for example, or to give them minimal pocket money and make them earn the rest. I have a friend who acts as a 'bank' to his kids, and gives them generous interest on their savings so they prefer to save rather than spend. There are lots of ways to teach kids about money. The important thing is to find ones that work for you and your kids.

And of course you've got to teach your children to make their own decisions. From which clothes to wear today when they're aged 2, through to which A-levels to take, they've got to learn to plan their own lives. And that means learning the consequences of making the wrong decisions too, so no interfering when you see them about to make a dreadful mistake. Of course you can suggest and advise – though as they get older you need to start waiting to be asked – but no pressure, OK? This is their life. Just remember, you're counting down to their 18th birthday, and after that, they're on their own . . .

> # THEY'VE GOT TO LEARN TO PLAN THEIR OWN LIVES. AND THAT MEANS LEARNING THE CONSEQUENCES OF MAKING THE WRONG DECISIONS TOO

RULE 26

Let them go (wild)

Remember the days when you used to leave the house in the morning and be off all day, and your parents didn't know where you were? Which was probably just as well because you were getting up to all sorts of things they probably wouldn't have wanted to know about. Building dens, play fighting with sticks, stealing milk, lighting fireworks, climbing trees, sticking slugs on next door's cat.

Kids need to do those things. They need it as much as they ever did. But parents are increasingly reluctant to allow it. We worry about physical damage, when the emotional damage of keeping them under wraps is far worse. Life is a series of risk assessments, and if children don't learn to take risks when they're young, they won't be equipped for coping with the rest of life.

I know your child could be seriously injured running around fields or hanging out with friends in the park. They could also be injured falling down stairs without ever leaving the house. For some reason, over the last couple of generations we've lost our sense of perspective on these things. The fact is that when kids go it alone, they take much more responsibility for monitoring their own safety, because they know you're not there to do it for them. So they learn far more. All children need to learn to climb trees, light fires, build dens, swing on ropes, and get wet with their clothes on. And yes, sometimes they come home with bumps and bruises, or blood running down their arm or leg, but they'll have learnt something for next time.*

I'll tell you something else I've noticed over the years, when I see kids being given a bit more freedom than normal. The ones whose parents are anxious are almost always the most nervous kids. They're unsure about how to look after themselves because

---

* Such as that cats have claws, and don't like being covered in slugs.

they've rarely been allowed to do it before. Whereas the kids with gung-ho parents are almost always the most confident ones. And actually, confidence is very important when it comes to looking after yourself. I know you're probably thinking that confidence sounds like a bad idea when facing risks, but that's *over*confidence you're thinking of. I'm talking about justified confidence.

If you hand a small child a cup and say, 'Careful, don't spill it' they're actually more likely to spill it than if you say nothing. You've made them anxious, and focused them on the risk. In the same way, confident children are more likely to make rational decisions than those who are apprehensive. So by cocooning your child you may think you're keeping them safe, but in the long run you're reducing their ability to take care of themselves.

> # THE CHILDREN WHOSE PARENTS ARE ANXIOUS ARE ALMOST ALWAYS THE MOST NERVOUS KIDS

RULE 27

Teach them to think for themselves

Not only do your kids have to make their own decisions (Rule 25), but they also need to be able to think for themselves. If your child argues with you, frustrating as it can be, at least it shows they're thinking independently. And that's what you want (although possibly you don't feel as if you want it right now).

I was with a friend the other day whose 5-year-old was being deliberately irritating, as 5-year-olds can. My friend got angry and the 5-year-old got upset at being told off. I was very impressed to hear my friend ask her daughter, 'Why do you think I'm cross with you?' The little girl thought about it, and mumbled, 'Because I didn't stop when you said stop'. Now she really wouldn't have questioned why her mother was angry if she hadn't been asked to. But her mother was teaching her to think.

My friend had grasped the single most basic technique for teaching children to think: ask them questions. It really doesn't matter whether you ask them why they prefer cricket to football, what they think would be the best way to cater for 100 people at a wedding, how to reduce global warming, or whether they think American foreign policy in the Middle East is right (maybe save this one for when they're a bit older). You just need to get them thinking.

And challenge their ideas. Not aggressively, but ask them, 'Why do you think that?' When they're 2 years old you can ask them why they think a dog barks. When they're 12 you can ask whether they think the price of designer trainers is justified. (And if not, why would they expect you to spend that much on shoes for them? Ah – Rule 25 – give them their own clothing allowance.)

Keep challenging and asking questions. Get them debating and arguing and justifying and questioning. And once they can do it instinctively without you having to kick them off with a question, you know you've mastered Rule 27.

> WHEN THEY'RE 2 YEARS OLD YOU CAN ASK THEM WHY THEY THINK A DOG BARKS. WHEN THEY'RE 12 YOU CAN ASK WHETHER THEY THINK THE PRICE OF DESIGNER TRAINERS IS JUSTIFIED

Use praise wisely

Well done! You've made it to Rule 28. You're nearly a quarter of the way to being a fully paid-up Rules parent.

I hope that made you feel encouraged – that's the purpose of praise. And we Rules parents know that if we're doing our job properly, our praise will be one of the biggest motivators for our kids. You wouldn't let their birthday go by without giving them a present, so don't let good achievements go by without giving them praise.

Ah, but it's not quite that simple, is it? How many parents do you know who don't use praise as wisely as they might? You have to give them the right amount, in the right way.

The expression, 'You can't have too much of a good thing' certainly doesn't apply to praise. That doesn't mean you should be stingy, but you should give praise in proportion to your child's achievements. If you over-praise them you devalue the currency. If you tell them they're superbly brilliant when they do something pretty average, what will you say when they do something really brilliant? And if every little thing they achieve is rewarded with copious praise, they'll be terrified of failing you. And they don't need that kind of pressure.

A lot of parents forget to praise their child for behaving well, because they take it for granted. But children really want to hear that you noticed how good they were: 'Well done for not picking your nose in front of Auntie Myrtle,' or 'You must be exhausted, but you're still managing not to moan. That's really good.' This is what persuades them that it's worth being good next time.

You can recognize your child's achievements with thanks as well as praise. That takes off some of the pressure, and allows you to acknowledge them without being effusive. What's more, it's a great way of reinforcing good behaviour, and reassuring them that you notice when they get things right, not just when they go wrong. 'Thanks for hanging up the towel after your bath.' 'Thanks for doing your homework without needing to be reminded.' 'It was good to come home to a tidy kitchen – thank you.'

Now, one last point about praise before you've mastered this Rule. Which of the following do you think your child would most like to hear: 'What a lovely drawing!' or 'What a lovely drawing – I do like the way you've managed to make the horse look as if it's really moving. How did you do that?' Yep – be specific with your praise if you can, and ask them questions too. That will really make them glow.

YOU HAVE TO GIVE
THEM THE RIGHT AMOUNT,
IN THE RIGHT WAY

RULE 29

Make sure they know what's important

Hang on – I haven't quite done with praise yet. OK, now we know how to give them praise effectively. But have you ever stopped to think about what you praise your child for? Think about it now.

I know parents who praise their children most frequently for winning things. In some cases it's sports, in others it's school work. I know others whose praise is largely focused on polite behaviour. Or looking beautifully turned out. Or being 'good'.

The things we choose to praise our children for tell them more about our values than almost anything else. This is how our children assess what really matters in life. If they get all the best responses from you for looking beautiful, or for winning, or for eating everything on their plate, this is what they will unconsciously assume is the most important thing. They'll put all their efforts into it in order to gain your approval, and will start out in life putting huge emphasis on these things.

This means you have a huge responsibility to praise them for the right things. If you always praise them for doing well at school but never for behaving well, what does that tell them about your values? Are you more likely to praise them for winning than for trying hard? No, of course you're not, you're a Rules parent. But a lot of other parents would.

That doesn't mean you can't ever say 'Well done' if they're pleased with themselves for coming top of the class, or winning their race. But be conscious of the balance you give them.

On the plus side, praise is a hugely effective way to imbue your children with the values that matter to you. Telling them, 'I was impressed by the way you took the trouble to include Ali in your group when she was feeling new and shy' impresses on your child that kindness and considerateness are important qualities. Like-wise, 'I admire the way you enrolled on that climbing course even though you were nervous', or 'It doesn't matter that you didn't come top – what I noticed was that you put in such a big effort'.

As a parent, it helps to be aware of the values that matter most to you, and to look out for opportunities to acknowledge those things in your child. It's a positive way to use praise (while still keeping it in proportion) to encourage your child to be hard-working, thoughtful, unselfish, courageous, determined and kind. And whatever else you think matters.

> # ARE YOU MORE LIKELY TO PRAISE THEM FOR WINNING THAN FOR TRYING HARD? NO, OF COURSE YOU'RE NOT, YOU'RE A RULES PARENT

RULE 30

Show them how to lose

This is the flipside to being measured about the praise you give. When kids do badly at something, they need to recognize the fact. Often, they're very well aware that they've messed up, and if you try to tell them it's fine, they know it's a lie. They may want to believe it, but deep down they'll know. So you just confuse them if you try to big them up with comments like:

- 'You had that cold just before the exam, so it's no wonder you didn't do so well.'

- 'Well, they shouldn't have let that girl compete in the under 12s. She's as tall as an adult.'

- 'The ref was biased. You should have won.'

That's not to say that you should tell them what rubbish they are, or how they've let you down (I know, of course you wouldn't do that). But how can they learn from their mistakes unless they accept them? You're not helping your child if you tell them they've nothing to learn and they were just a victim of fate – they was robbed.

You can give them a measured opinion if you like. You could say, 'You didn't do brilliantly, but you did respectably' – something like that (if it's true). But you don't necessarily need to give an opinion at all. What's more helpful is to get them to see where they could have done better. So try asking questions: 'How did you feel that went?' is always a good one to start with, not least because *you* may be disappointed that they didn't win, but *they* may be really chuffed to have come fifth. In which case you can let them enjoy what they perceive as success.

If they're unhappy with their performance though, ask them why they think they didn't do better. If they try to blame the ref, the teacher, the other kids, gently point out that they're avoiding the real issue.

Ask your child what they're going to do next time. Remember that they don't have to be competitive. Sometimes, the best answer is to stop competing, or to care less when they do badly, or to enjoy the match/exercise/process and not be so focused on the result. But of course there are times when they will really want to win. In which case they can train harder, or get more sleep the night before, or practise their leg spins more often, or put in more revision. It's easier to cope with losing if you start to visualize how you can change things next time. And it helps you to see that at least some elements of success are within your control.

Another useful question is to ask your child who they think deserved to win or to come top. If you can encourage them to be honest like this, they'll often recognize that the result was right. And they'll see who they can learn from for next time.

Once your child has got a balanced view of where they went wrong, and how to avoid such disappointment next time, you can find something good to say that's genuine. 'You may not have been the fastest, but you certainly showed great determination.' Remembering, of course, that it's important what you praise them for.

> # IF THEY'RE UNHAPPY WITH THEIR PERFORMANCE, ASK THEM WHY THEY THINK THEY DIDN'T DO BETTER

RULE 31

Know the value of boundaries

I watched a neighbour of mine once as her 4-year-old jumped up onto the wall surrounding their front garden and ran along it. This might not sound so bad, but on the other side of the wall was a 15 ft drop to a concrete parking area. I must have looked horrified because she clocked my reaction and said, 'I know. I've told him not to but he just ignores me. What can you do?' Well, I was so speechless I didn't actually answer her. (Besides, if I'd told her she'd just have ignored me.)

You know as well as I do that the answer to her question was, 'Say no and mean it'. It was a particularly graphic example of how children need boundaries – in this case for the poor little chap's personal safety. Actually, this child was a prime example of what happens when you don't give kids clear boundaries. He was known (out of earshot of his family) as the 'feral child' because he was wild. He was constantly pushing to see how far he could go, and apparently there wasn't a limit.

The feral child misbehaved appallingly, had very few friends, and must have thought his parents didn't care about him at all. After all, if they had, would they have let him run along a wall with a 15 ft drop? Would they have allowed him to behave as he pleased without ever paying him attention, no matter what he did?

The world is a scary place when you're a child. It's also pretty scary when you're an adult. The best security children have is a clear set of rules and guidelines so they can be sure they're staying within safe limits. They test boundaries constantly, especially when they're little, not because they want to extend them, but because they want to *make sure they haven't moved*. Your job is to make those boundaries clear to them and guarantee that they'll stay put. So you say no to them every time they climb up on the wall, and if necessary you lift them down to enforce the rule. That way you'll have a safe, confident, happy child who knows where they stand, can learn about the world around them because it doesn't keep shifting, and who knows you love them.

And by the way, that means both of you (if you're not a single parent). It's no good if one parent enforces the boundaries and the other doesn't – that just confuses the kids more. You have to share the hard cop role (more on this in Rule 38). It doesn't matter if the odd detail varies (maybe Daddy always lets them sit on his lap for stories while Mummy likes them to snuggle down under the covers). But for all significant rules, both of you must enforce the boundaries if you want happy and confident kids.

> **BOTH OF YOU MUST ENFORCE THE BOUNDARIES IF YOU WANT HAPPY AND CONFIDENT KIDS**

RULE 32

Bribery doesn't have to be bad

Boy, has bribery got a bad name with parents. It's reckoned to be one of the worst things you can do. But hang on a minute – let's define bribery first, shall we? Suppose your child is behaving appallingly and you tell them you'll give them a tenner to shut up and behave. Well, OK – that, I grant you, is bribery. We won't do that, obviously.

How about this one then? Your child is behaving perfectly *at the moment* but you suspect it may not last. Maybe you're about to drag them off to the shops, or make them do their homework, tidy their room, eat their greens, turn off the TV, go to bed or do something else that generally elicits a bad response. You tell them you'll reward them in some way if they continue to behave well. Do you reckon that's bribery?

I don't. And I'll tell you why. When I used to work in big organizations, they were always telling me that if I coped with this responsibility I'd get promotion, or if I performed to a certain standard I'd get a bonus. I can't see the difference. They didn't call it bribery, mind you, they called it incentivization. And it was considered a Good Thing.

So let's have none of this nonsense about not incentivizing children. So long as you do it before the bad behaviour starts, it's a very sensible approach.

Of course, you want to be careful about the kind of incentives you give. If you always use money, you send out a depressing message to your kids about how the world works. Not to mention ending up skint. And you want the size of the incentive to match the size of the demand you're making in response. Don't buy them a whole new wardrobe to reward them for hanging up half a dozen items of clothing.

Ideally, you'll make the reward fit the request. If they're good all the time you're at the shops, you'll take them to the park afterwards. If they can get themselves out of bed in the morning without you having to pour a bucket of cold water over them, you'll make their bedtime 15 minutes later. If they keep their room tidy for two months you'll increase their clothing allowance.

And you haven't forgotten the best reward of all, have you? Of course you haven't. Your kids will do a hell of a lot for free if they know they'll get your approval at the end of it. So you don't have to concede a dozen incentives a day; most of the time they'll be very happy to hear, 'I'd be really pleased/impressed/happy if you'd . . .'. And make sure you remember to tell them afterwards how pleased/impressed/happy you are.

> # IDEALLY, YOU'LL MAKE THE REWARD FIT THE REQUEST

RULE 33

Moods are catching

When you have kids you become a family. No longer are you a free spirit or a cosy couple. You're a family. And everyone in a family interacts with everyone else. That means everyone's moods affect everyone else. Now, some people are better than others at being cheerful when everyone around them is throwing a hissy fit, but most of us find that our moods change with the moods of the people around us.

As a Rules parent, you need to understand that you are responsible for the family's mood. I don't mean it's your fault every time someone is unhappy. I just mean that if everyone has subsided into gloom, or if you all start shouting at one another, it's no good wishing one of the others would stop whingeing or yelling or sulking or complaining or niggling or bickering. If you think someone should snap out of it and set a better tone, it had better be you.

Kids don't understand that moods are catching. They have no idea that the reason you're so irritable is because they've been winding you up all day. Sure, you can start teaching them, but it will be years before they do anything about it. As soon as they feel down they'll act miserable to punish you, even if they know it will drag you down too. 'That'll teach 'em', they'll think. No, it takes an adult to break that kind of pattern. And that's you, like I said.

One of my children in particular (better not say which one) used to clash with me constantly when he was younger. What really drove me mad about him was that he would never back down, even if I lost my temper with him. Eventually my wife – picking her moment carefully – pointed out that perhaps it might have something to do with the fact that I never backed down either. The example I was setting him was teaching him an unhelpful way of resolving conflict.

Look, the facts aren't necessarily pleasant but here they are: parents who yell at their children are more likely to have children who yell. Parents who sulk with their kids encourage kids to sulk. Parents who always moan tend to have moany kids. Not every time, but far more often than they otherwise would. Or what can happen instead, depending on personality, is that they go to the other extreme and instead of being angry like you (say), they'll get really upset if anybody ever gets angry, or at least have 'issues', as they say, around anger. If you want your child to handle their moods maturely, you have to be mature in the way you handle yours. Of course, that's the plus side. You can influence your child's moods – and the way they deal with them – for the better. And that creates an upward spiral for everyone.

> # THE FACTS AREN'T NECESSARILY PLEASANT BUT HERE THEY ARE: PARENTS WHO YELL AT THEIR CHILDREN HAVE CHILDREN WHO YELL

You're setting their eating patterns for life

I'm not about to tell you what you should feed your kids. I've no idea. You might be a vegan, you might be addicted to doughnuts (I could understand that) or be phobic about alfalfa. It's up to you to decide how to feed your kids responsibly, and there are lots of healthy diets you could choose as well as the obviously unhealthy ones to avoid (like the doughnuts, sadly).

But whatever the actual food you feed them, the way your children eat will set up habits they will find it very hard to break, so make sure you give them good habits. That is to say, habits that will enable them easily to enjoy a healthy adulthood.

I was brought up in an age when eating habits were very different. My mother's generation had lived through a war, had experienced rationing, and obesity was rare. As a result, many of the habits I was given made sense to my mother but they didn't turn out to make sense for me.

For example, I was expected to eat everything on my plate. I wasn't allowed to leave the table until I did. That was fine as a small boy when portions were small, but as I got older it did nothing for my weight. Even when I really wanted to lose weight, I found it almost impossible to leave food on my plate. Now my children are expected to eat what they help themselves to, but if they're served more food than they can manage, they're allowed to leave it.

Here's another example. As a child, I didn't get pudding until I'd eaten my main course. What did that teach me? That sweet, stodgy puddings are where it's at, and savoury food is just a purgatory you have to get through to reach that sticky, sugary goal. That hasn't helped me maintain a healthy weight either, I can tell you. How do I get round it with my kids? We almost never have puddings, except when we have people over, and of course they aren't necessarily expected to finish all their main course anyway.

How about this one? I was given a sweet if I hurt myself, or as a reward if I was really good. There's another one that's hung like a millstone round my neck. Whenever I feel down, I reward myself with a Mars bar. I tell myself that when I've finished writing this group of Rules, I can have a piece of cake.

What patterns are you setting up for your kids? Maybe your children are genetically guaranteed never to have a weight problem or any other health problems associated with bad diet. Maybe your kids need a completely different set of habits from mine. Maybe you have better ways than me of avoiding the patterns I've just described. I don't have all the answers here. All I'm saying is be aware of the habits that you're giving them, and make sure they're the ones you want them to have.

THE WAY YOUR CHILDREN EAT WILL SET UP HABITS THEY WILL FIND IT VERY HARD TO BREAK

Communicate

It's so easy as parents to miss the kids out of the loop. To begin with, they're too small to understand. As they get bigger you've got out of the habit, and anyway, it's just one more layer of complication to include them. Ah yes, but it's also one more step towards an integrated family that operates smoothly as a team (at least on a good day).

So what am I banging on about this time? What sort of communication? Well, let me give you a couple of examples. Do you always remember to tell your kids when a visitor is expected? You probably do if it's someone they're excited about seeing, but what if it's someone they don't even know? Someone measuring up for a new sofa cover, or mending the washing machine. Do you tell your toddler every time you put them in the car where you're going? It's obvious to you, but not to them.

And don't forget that communication works two ways. Yes, you've got to tell your team what's going on (and ideally why) but you also need to ask for their input and actually listen to the response. Do you consult with your children about where you go on holiday? By the time they're teenagers they'll probably give you an opinion without waiting to be asked, but what about when they're aged 6 or 7?

What about when you change your car? Do you ask the kids for their views? OK, you're not going to buy a Lamborghini just because they want one, but you can ask what matters to them – plenty of room in the back, a roofrack for the surfboard, a sunroof. After all, if they've had their say, they're much more likely to be happy with what you finally choose.

If you manage all the above every time, full marks to you. In fact, you should be writing this book, not me, because I still don't always remember. But I remember often enough to see how much difference it makes to the kids to feel included and part of the family. And, actually, they can be damned useful too if they know what's going on. They're full of ideas which, OK, need a lot of sifting, but in among them can be some really useful suggestions I'd never have come up with otherwise.

DO YOU TELL YOUR TODDLER EVERY TIME YOU PUT THEM IN THE CAR WHERE YOU'RE GOING? IT'S OBVIOUS TO YOU, BUT NOT TO THEM

Set clear targets

Here's a Rule I picked up from the business world, and a really good one too. Good managers are always on about setting targets and working towards specified goals. And they're absolutely right. It's very demoralising if your boss tells you, 'Sell more!' You've no idea whether the extra 10 per cent sales you've managed this month will disappoint them or astound them. And you kinda figure that they have no idea either, otherwise they'd have told you, 'Sell 10 per cent more!'

So we all know from work that clear targets feel good, you know what's expected of you, and you feel that your boss cares about your performance. OK then, why do we tell our kids, 'Keep your room tidier', or 'Clean out the rabbit more often', or 'Don't spend so long on that computer'?

Can't you just hear the implication that you're not really as bothered as you're making out? Which sounds more convincing to you: 'Don't spend so long on that computer' or 'You can have two hours a day on the computer'? And which is easier for your child to understand?

Sometimes we really aren't trying hard enough, but sometimes we just don't stop to think about whether our child will know what we mean. 'Clean the rabbit out more often' might seem perfectly explicit to you, but they might be clueless as to what you actually want. Does it mean clean it once a week or once a month? Or give it fresh hay twice a week and change the sawdust every fortnight? You have to specify if you want your kids to feel motivated to do as you ask, and to feel as if you care. And – most importantly – actually to do what you're asking.

This rule was really brought home to me several years ago when I asked one of my kids to tidy her room. When I went upstairs later I found the room almost as messy as before. When I started to chastise her for this she looked really hurt and said, 'But I have tidied it. Look!' In fact she had picked up everything off the floor . . . and that was it. But she honestly thought that was what I wanted. That's when I realized it was my own fault, and not only was the room not tidy but I wasn't being fair on her either.

SOMETIMES WE REALLY
AREN'T TRYING HARD
ENOUGH, BUT SOMETIMES
WE JUST DON'T
STOP TO THINK

Don't be a nag

I read a very interesting piece recently about someone who had been researching into nagging (I wonder how many times they had to be asked). They discovered that if you nag people, they're actually *less* likely to do what you want than if you don't.

So how do you get your kids to do things if you don't nag? Well, nagging has a tone to it that implies irritation and that's what's so off-putting about it. And when nagging gets really bad – and this is something Rules parents make sure they never do – you nag children about what they *are* rather than simply about what they do. So 'You didn't shut the door' is a reasonable reprimand, but 'You never shut the door' is a nag. Even worse is condemning their natural character: 'You never think about anyone else' or 'You're just clumsy.' If you do this to your kids, you'll make them worse. And who can blame them?

But there's no need to use any irritable tone or personal phrases. All you have to do is ask firmly, and make it clear what will happen if they don't do it. Like this: 'Please do your homework. If it isn't done by 6 o'clock I'll have to turn the computer off until you've done it.' Then keep quiet until 6 o'clock and, if necessary, turn off the computer. If this is your standard approach, it won't take long for your kids to realize you're not joking.

I visited someone's house once for lunch, and the kitchen table where we were going to eat was covered in children's toys, drawings, sweets, Lego bricks, playing cards and general assorted trash. I offered (somewhat nervously) to clear it. 'Oh no,' replied my host, 'there's no need. The children will do it'. I wondered how on earth she was going to get the kids to clear the table before the vegetables came to the boil when they were engrossed in something else, but she went to the kitchen door and called cheerfully, 'Everything that's still on the kitchen table in 10 minutes is going in the bin!' Clearly used to this – and clearly having been persuaded at some time in the past that she wasn't bluffing – the children all appeared instantly and five minutes later the table was ready for lunch. No nagging – she just said it once and made sure they knew what would happen if they ignored her.

There's something else worth saying about nagging, and that is that children go through a long period of several years where they can do certain jobs but it's not reasonable to expect them to remember it for themselves. So instead of being cross that your child has forgotten yet again to feed the hamster, and being tempted to nag them, it's much happier all round if you regard it as part of the deal that they feed the hamster but it's your job to remind them to do it. Now you just need someone to nag you to remember.

> # THERE'S NO NEED TO USE ANY IRRITABLE TONE OR PERSONAL PHRASES

DISCIPLINE
RULES

I don't know about you, but I don't like the word 'discipline'. It implies telling off, punishment, even (heaven forbid) beating. Children should be seen and not heard – all that stuff.

Actually, though, once you get over the word itself, it's a handy essential skill for parents. If you get the discipline thing right, it is so much easier being a parent, and being a child. Yes, your kids benefit hugely from good discipline. We already looked at the value of boundaries (Rule 31), and discipline is about how to enforce those boundaries. When it works well, there should never be any need for telling off, punishment or beating. And then everyone's happy.

Present a united front

If you asked your boss for an extra day's holiday and they said 'No', you'd be disappointed but you'd put up with it. After all, it's not as if you're entitled to it. But suppose you then asked your boss's boss, who said 'Yes, of course, no problem'. Now where does that leave you all?

You're not sure whether it's OK to take a day off or not. But you are sure that your boss's opinion doesn't count for much. And if your boss ever says no to you again, you know where to go. In fact, maybe just bypass your boss completely next time. Meanwhile your boss feels belittled and frustrated, probably angry with their boss, and knows they've lost your respect. And your boss's boss finds they've lost the respect of your boss, and set themselves up to be brought every future request and expected to look kindly on them all.

Confused? I'm not surprised. Inconsistent discipline from both parents leads to all sorts of confusion, frustration and undermining of respect. Whereas if your boss's boss had backed up your boss, it would all have been so simple.

You have to understand that when you undermine your partner, you are not being kind to your child so they will love you more (yes, admit it, that's the bottom line). You are actually confusing them and undermining their respect for both of you, and their confidence in those all-important boundaries.

If you're a single parent, you're not off the hook. This still applies every time there's someone else sharing responsibility for the children. Your parents when they go on holiday with you, or your childminder, or your friend who looks after them on Tuesday afternoons after school.

If you want your child to feel secure, you have to back each other up. And that means sharing the hard cop role too. It's worth it:

they'll feel happier, clearer about boundaries, and they'll respect (and love) you both for it. Eventually.

Of course, you don't have to agree every tiny possible rule in advance – when it comes to the detail you only have to agree that whatever one of you says, the other will back up if asked: 'If Daddy says no then the answer's no.' The crucial thing to understand is that, apart from the big stuff that you should have agreed in advance (Rule 13), the fact that you agree is more important than what you're agreeing about.

> # THE FACT THAT YOU AGREE IS MORE IMPORTANT THAN WHAT YOU'RE AGREEING ABOUT

Carrots beat sticks

Can you remember being a kid? Go on, think back – of course you can. Now, suppose your teacher said you'd get a gold star/distinction/sweet/pick of the stationery cupboard if you did well in your next spelling test. Now suppose that instead of that, they warned you that if you did badly you'd be kept in at breaktime/given detention/banned from games (or made to do double games, depending on your natural sporting inclinations). Which one of these would make you most likely to do well?

Well, if you were anything like me, you'd have a fat chance of doing well in any spelling test. But I'd certainly have tried harder for the reward. And so would you, if you're typical. According to modern researchers and child psychologists, carrots are far more effective for encouraging kids to co-operate.

That doesn't mean that you have to reward your children every time they say please, or pay them for tidying their room. Most of the time they'll be happy just to know that you've noticed their efforts and appreciate them. So let them know: 'That was a nice thank you', or 'Hey, you tidied your room before I'd even asked you to. Brilliant!' Or, 'Thanks for being quiet this morning so I could have a lie-in'. Now they're going to want to do it again so they can get your praise again. It's vital that they know you've noticed, so you have to remember to tell them or it won't work (and you'll be woken at 6am next Sunday by the sound of squabbling).

When it comes to bigger stuff that you discuss with them in advance, it's still important to use carrots and not sticks. Tell them they'll get their favourite supper if they're really good in the park, or promise them an increase in their clothing allowance if they keep their room tidy for a whole month.

That's not to say that sticks don't have their place (metaphorically, obviously), but in an ideal world they'd be in the background and never get used. They're for serious lapses of behaviour but, even so, they should always be used in conjunction with carrots. So you can tell your teenager that if they keep coming home late they'll be grounded for a weekend, but if they make it home by the agreed time for a whole month you'll extend the curfew by 15 minutes.

Just one word of warning here (mustn't make it too easy for you). Beware of putting too much pressure on your kids by offering substantial rewards if your child might not succeed. If you promise them their own car or a share of yours if they get certain A-level results, you're piling on the pressure. And they'll end up being punished twice if they don't make it. Once by feeling they've failed, and again by not having a car to drive.

> IT'S VITAL THAT THEY
> KNOW YOU'VE NOTICED,
> SO YOU HAVE TO
> REMEMBER TO
> TELL THEM

RULE 40

Be consistent

When I was a kid, I could answer my mum back one day and she'd laugh and tell me she was pleased I could stand up for myself. Next day I could say the same thing and get walloped for it. And there was never any clue to which way she'd go. This applied not only to giving her backchat, but to most other things too. It meant I spent a lot of my time walking on eggshells.

It also meant I had no idea what was and wasn't allowed – it seemed to be decided on some kind of secret lottery basis which I wasn't privy to. So there was little point in regulating my behaviour. After all, I might get into trouble, but then again I might not. It generally seemed worth the risk – certainly to me.

Your kids are just the same. They need to know what is and isn't acceptable. And they judge that by what was and wasn't OK yesterday and the day before. If they're not getting a consistent message, they're clueless as to how they have to behave, and those all-important boundaries (Rule 31 again) aren't being properly maintained. That means the kids feel confused, insecure and perhaps even unloved.

I'll tell you the toughest thing about this Rule: it means that a lot of the time you can't break the rules even when you want to. It's just not fair on the kids. If you've decided that you don't allow the kids to sleep in your bed with you, you have to stick to it (unless you're prepared to change the rule permanently). Just because your little one was a bit sad about something today, and they're so warm and snuggly and smelling of bathtime, and you're feeling a bit down yourself anyway . . . no, no, no! Stop right there! Let them into your bed once and it will be ten times harder to say no to them next time, and they won't understand why. Say no now (softly and with an extra hug) and you're only being cruel to be kind (to yourself as well as them).

Did you notice back there I said 'unless you're prepared to change the rule permanently'? Of course, changing the rules is always an option. You might suddenly realize that life would be altogether sweeter if your child shared your bed every night, and you don't know why you ever banned it in the first place. Well, you can change the rule (though best check with your partner first), but once you've changed it, you have to stick with it for a long time. Your kids will get just as confused if the rule changes every month as they will if it changes every night. So how long do you have to stick to the new version of the rule? If not permanently, at least until your kids have forgotten that it was ever different. And the older they get, the longer that will take.

I'LL TELL YOU THE TOUGHEST THING ABOUT THIS RULE: A LOT OF THE TIME YOU CAN'T BREAK THE RULES EVEN WHEN YOU WANT TO

Lighten up

As a teenager I was once helping prepare a family meal (I use the word 'helping' loosely, as you'll see). My mother was actually cooking the meal, but I got the frozen peas out for her. For some reason I cannot justify, I held the peas up by the top corner of the packet, and used the scissors to cut off the corner, just below the level of my finger and thumb. Predictably the whole packet (apart from the corner remaining in my fingers) hit the ground and frozen peas rocketed across the floor – under the fridge, the cooker, the washing machine, and our feet.

Horrified, I looked up at my mother, who was already under pressure trying to carve the meat, stop the gravy burning and cook the vegetables, waiting for the inevitable haranguing[*] . . . But instead, my mother was doubled up with laughter.

And you know what? I've never made that mistake since (yes, I know most people manage to go through life without making that particular mistake at all). The point is that I didn't need to be told off in order to learn from my mistake. It did far more for my view of my mother and for our relationship to have her laugh than to have her tell me how stupid I was (which, frankly, was pretty damn obvious anyway).

Of course it was a complete accident, however stupid. What about those times your kids are deliberately winding you up or answering you back? Even then, you can often turn trouble into fun. If you can crack a joke, or tease them in a gentle and affectionate way at the right moment, you can often break their resolve to make your life miserable for the next five minutes. And you'll all have more fun, and a stronger relationship, as a result.

---

[*] This is not a word I should have attempted, having just told you how rubbish my spelling was. Whichever way you spell this, it looks wrong. Hopefully by the time you read it, my editor will have corrected it.

There's a terrific kids' book by John Burningham called *Would You Rather . . .?* It asks kids if they would rather, for example, be covered in jam, or water, or dragged through the mud by a dog? (I thoroughly recommend it, by the way. The book I mean, not being dragged through the mud.) My younger kids love it and sometimes, when they're just starting to misbehave, I can defuse things by asking them, 'Would you rather . . . stop it right now, be sent to your room for five minutes, or be tickled mercilessly for 30 seconds?' It makes them giggle and distracts them from whatever they were about to do, and they seem to appreciate the fact that they're being stopped without being told off. Now I come to think about it, I know some adults I should try it on too.

LIGHTEN UP . . . YOU'LL
ALL HAVE MORE FUN,
AND A STRONGER
RELATIONSHIP

Focus on the problem, not the person

I used to know a rather worthy, earnest type of person who did a child behaviour course or some such thing. On one occasion she told us that she'd learnt this vital principle: 'He's not a naughty boy, he's a good boy who's done a naughty thing.' Well, we thought this was one of the funniest examples of politically correct psychology gone mad that we'd ever heard, and we missed no opportunity to send up this absurdly saccharine piece of advice.

The embarrassing thing, though, is that actually I have to admit she was absolutely right. I'm still not beyond taking the mickey out of the phrase itself ('It's not a naughty computer, it's a good computer that's done a naughty thing') but with much pride-swallowing I have to concede that the underlying principle couldn't be more spot on.

Once you tell a child that they are naughty, selfish, lazy, fat, stupid, rude, pushy, careless or anything else, you label them. And if they believe that label (and why shouldn't they – they're trained to believe what we tell them), they will start to live up to it. They'll think, 'There's no point my making an effort, I know I'm lazy'. Or 'What have I got to lose? They've got me down as naughty anyway'. Of course, this won't be a conscious thought process, at least not when they're small. But if you give them a label, they'll live up to it.

What you have to do is condemn their behaviour, not them. You can tell them, 'That's a selfish thing to do', or 'It's very rude to push in'. That way you're not passing comment on them, but only on their behaviour. If at this point you feel like shouting, 'But he *is* lazy!' I'm not telling you you're wrong, though it would be very un-PC of me to admit you could be right. I'm just saying that you should never, ever say so in front of them, or anyone else in case it gets back to them. Save it for your most private thoughts after the third time in a row they go out without even clearing the table, let alone helping you wash up.

Positive labels are a different thing entirely. So long as they're accurate (don't pressure your child by making them live up to something they can't), they likewise encourage your child to behave like their label – thoughtful, careful, brave or whatever.

And actually, you can sometimes use these positive labels to re-inforce good behaviour when they've lapsed: 'I was really surprised to see you behave so rudely. I always think of you as a particularly polite person.' It reassures them you haven't given up on your positive view of them, so it's not too late to live up to the 'polite' label.

WHAT YOU HAVE TO DO IS CONDEMN THEIR BEHAVIOUR, NOT THEM

Don't paint yourself into a corner

Oh, I'm dreadful at this one. It comes of being a spontaneous person (that's my excuse). I come out with these things and then – bang! Before I know it I've made some kind of daft threat I can't possibly see through. Not long ago I banned my son from watching TV for a whole year. Clearly unworkable, out of all proportion to the offence, and not in anyone's interests. How do you get out of that one?*

Fortunately, however, I'm not here to tell you to be like me. I'm just passing on what I've learnt from watching other parents, many of them more accomplished than I am. I do know when I'm getting this one wrong, and I am much better than I used to be (apart from the TV thing). And, as you know, that's the key to being a Rules parent – we know when we have more to learn, and we keep working at it.

Of course, the big problem with banning TV for a year is that the *real* rule about threats is that you have to carry them out. If you tell your child they can't get the stickle bricks out until they've put away the marbles, you have to make sure you follow it through. Otherwise, obviously, they'll never take any notice of your threats once they discover they're hollow.

A friend of mine never used to carry out threats and had rather out of control children as a result. After an enlightening conversation with a wise friend, he decided to try a different approach. On a family holiday he threatened his son, 'If you don't stop that, you won't be going surfing tomorrow'. Son thinks: 'Ha, course I will – Dad never does what he says, and if I don't go surfing, somebody else would have to stay home to look after me.'

---

* For the answer to this, see Rule 45.

What he didn't realize was that his dad had resolved to see the threat through. So when the behaviour continued, the dad followed through and missed the surfing himself in order to show he meant it. Not only did his son miss the surfing, but he spent the whole day with an extremely grumpy dad as he too was missing out because of his son's behaviour. Needless to say it was very effective, and my friend was encouraged to carry out his threats in future.

So always carry out your threats and, therefore, don't paint yourself into a corner with a threat you can't or won't see through. Think before you speak (note to self: must work harder at this one).

THEY'LL NEVER TAKE ANY NOTICE OF YOUR THREATS ONCE THEY DISCOVER THEY'RE HOLLOW

If you lose your temper, you're the loser

Our children learn their behaviour by watching ours. If we say please and thank you, they learn to do it too (in time). If we treat other people politely, they'll do the same thing. If we snort crack cocaine before breakfast, they'll think that's normal. And if we lose our temper when other people don't do as we want them to, they'll think that's the correct behaviour.

Most of the time it's pretty easy to behave as we want our children to. But when your blood pressure starts to rise, that's when the example you set is so critical – just when it's hardest to set a good example (damn). So how do you deal with your child when they argue with you? Do you manage to stay calm, not raise your voice, and listen to what they have to say? It's not easy, God knows, but it's the only way to get the same response back from them.

In most couples, for some reason, one is much more prone to lose their temper with the kids than the other. If this is you, don't feel a failure – your behaviour is very normal. But you do need to understand that every time you lose your rag with the kids, you effectively sanction their angry response. And that makes you the loser. It also won't help their future relationships if they grow up thinking that shouting gets you what you want, and is the standard way to handle conflict.

The same applies, by the way, to smacking. Whatever your opinion about smacking, the fact is that it doesn't work. It sends your kids the message that, sometimes at least, hitting people is the way to get what you want. If you do it in the heat of the moment, you let them know that you've lost control. That's pretty scary for kids, as well as indicating that it's OK to lose control and be aggressive. If you do it in cold blood, that shows you've thought it through and come to a considered opinion that aggression is the answer.

If you're going to smack your kids a lot, you'll damage them emotionally and you may turn them into bullies. If you're hardly ever going to smack them, why do it at all? My view, at least with certain children, is that if you started smacking them, when would you stop? If your child needs a good smack now and again, they're definitely the kind of child that should never be smacked. Rules parents don't need to smack their children.

So what if you can feel the bile rising and you know you're about to blow? Learn to recognize the signs as early as possible while you still have time to choose a different response. Failing that, run. Fast if necessary. Activate Rule 9. Get out of the situation until you can hack it – call it 'time out' for parents. If you have little ones, make sure they're safe (if necessary pick them up and put them somewhere safe) and then retire to a safe distance – out of earshot if necessary – until you have calmed down and can trust yourself to re-enter the fray. By which time they may well have got over their moment of rebellion anyway.

> IF YOUR CHILD NEEDS A GOOD SMACK NOW AND AGAIN, THEY'RE DEFINITELY THE KIND OF CHILD THAT SHOULD NEVER BE SMACKED

Apologize if you get it wrong

One of the things that should be coming through by now[*] is that the way we behave is the strongest model our kids have for their own behaviour. We've said that if you don't want them to lose their temper, you mustn't lose yours, and if you want them to say please and thank you, you must be as polite to them. Well, now here's another of those things you have to be able to do with your kids, and funnily enough lots of parents seem to have a problem with this one.

I guess the feeling is that if you admit you were wrong, you undermine your child's confidence in your all-powerfulness. If you say sorry, they'll realize you're not always perfect. Well, I've got news for you. It's only a matter of time before they work this out for themselves. You might as well let them down gently by showing them, now and again, that you're not God and you do make mistakes.

The more ready you are to apologize when you're wrong, the more your kids will see that it's not belittling to admit to being wrong – grown-ups they admire can do it readily. And they'll also see that everyone makes mistakes and it's nothing to be ashamed of. Aware of, yes, and ready to put it right, but not shaming. You need your kids to regard saying sorry as something they instinctively do as soon as they realize they've hurt, offended, inconvenienced or upset anyone.

I might add that some adults have a problem apologizing to anyone, let alone their kids. If you have a problem admitting when you're wrong, you need to address this now, before you bring your

---

[*] I'm assuming you're reading this book in order, and not starting here.

kids up to emulate you.* Parenthood is a great time for getting tough on your own shortcomings before you pass them down the generations.

Remember back in Rule 43 I banned my son from watching TV for a year? The only way out of this one was to tell him straight: 'I'm sorry I made a mistake. I lost my temper, which I shouldn't have done, and as a result I issued an absurd threat. What I should have said is that you can't watch TV for a week so, as you continued to be rude to me, that's what will actually happen.' Humiliating, possibly, but then I brought it on myself.

> ## YOU NEED YOUR KIDS TO REGARD SAYING SORRY AS SOMETHING THEY INSTINCTIVELY DO

---

* I realize that, by definition, if this is you, you won't want to admit it. I'm just trusting that you're enough of a Rules Player to start somewhere. Come on! You can do it . . .

Let them back in

OK, so you've had a row with your child. Maybe you handled it well, or maybe not (you're only human). But you're a Rules parent anyhow, so it can't have been that bad. Your child, on the other hand, was well out of order and sent to their room.

What happens next? This is critical, and I've made it a Rule because I've seen parents get this horribly wrong. Their child comes back downstairs, contrite, even apologetic, and their parent lays into them again about how badly they've behaved. Next thing they're on the defensive, arguing back, and sent to their room again. Or maybe the parent just stops speaking to them for a while and goes into a sulk.

Either way you're not allowing the child to escape from the bad feelings that they've just been trying to come to terms with. I recently heard a parent say to a child who apologized to them, 'The important thing is not to apologize. The important thing is not to do it again'. Quite true, of course, but not the time to say it. The poor child obviously felt he was still in trouble and unforgiven, and I could see his face crumple.

The most important thing of all is for your child to know that you still love them. They also need to know that there's some point in apologizing and determining to modify their behaviour. If you're still angry with them, why did they bother? So when the fight is over, let them know they're loved and welcomed back into your affection. And that you appreciate their apology and their ability to recognize that they were (at least partly) responsible for the fight.

Of course, you may well feel that you need to talk over the issue with your child – either the subject matter of the argument, or the way they handled it. But don't do it right now. Save it for later, once your friendship is firmly re-established. With older kids, you might want to say that it needs discussing later, or you might just want to bring it up at a better time – in the car together (you've got them trapped then), or maybe at bedtime. But not in front of anyone else who wasn't involved – family or siblings or friends.

If you know you're one of those people who likes to talk things to death, resist the temptation to go over the fight unless it's really necessary, especially with teenagers. Most kids know perfectly well what they did wrong, and talking it over every time there's a row will just bug them. It's not an easy thing for them to do, so don't put them through it unless it's really necessary. Of course, you may still need to resolve the original issue, but save this until you're both feeling jollier.

> ## THE MOST IMPORTANT THING OF ALL IS FOR YOUR CHILD TO KNOW THAT YOU STILL LOVE THEM

The right of expression

You may feel that you have an easier life when your kids are on an even keel. No rows, no tears, no outbursts. You're quite right, it's much easier. But it's not good for kids to be like that all the time. They have strong emotions and they need to be able to show them. When they're angry, they have to be allowed to say so. Your job is to teach them to say so in an acceptable way, and not to conceal their feelings no matter what.

I've known families where the kids get told off for being angry, regardless of how they do it. Of course, they must learn to be angry without being aggressive, abusive or threatening, but they must still be allowed to feel angry and to say so. Anger can be justified, anyway, and your kids have to know they can express justified anger without being told off for it. They need to hear, 'I can see exactly why you're angry, but it still isn't OK to swear at your sister.'

A child that isn't allowed to express their feelings won't be able to get rid of them – even grown-ups struggle with that one. All the child can do is bottle them up, and that can lead to emotional and even physical problems. What's more, they'll grow into an adult who can't say how they feel, which can be hugely damaging in all sorts of relationships, especially close partnerships.

People who have grown up without rows may not understand that if you row it can still be alright afterwards. So they're afraid to argue with their partner in case their partner walks out on them. That means problems aren't aired, resentments build up, feelings are bottled up, and all that stuff we know isn't healthy.

I know we're still in the discipline section of this book (just), but while we're on the subject of expressing feelings, I just want to stress how good it is for kids to cry. And adults, come to that. Not many parents discipline their kids for crying, but I've heard plenty tell their child, 'Don't be a baby', or 'Come on, it's not that bad'. Well, obviously it feels that bad to them, or they wouldn't be crying, would they? They'll learn soon enough at school not to cry when it's inappropriate, so you don't need to worry about that. I learnt many years ago from a very dear friend that the correct response when someone is crying (this goes for adults, too) is not 'There, there, don't cry', but 'That's it. Let it out. Let it all out'.

A CHILD THAT ISN'T ALLOWED TO EXPRESS THEIR FEELINGS WON'T BE ABLE TO GET RID OF THEM

PERSONALITY RULES

Ask anyone who has more than one child (yourself, quite possibly) and they'll tell you that they're all different. They can have the same biological parents, grow up in the same family, go to the same school, take the same holidays, but they'll be completely different people.

And that has implications for the way you bring them up. Your aim is to bring out their individuality, not to mould them into something you want them to be. Well, you know that, you're a Rules parent after all. But how do you do it? That's what this next group of Rules is about. Follow these and you'll enable your kids to grow up into the wonderful, independent, self-assured, free-thinking people they were always meant to be.

RULE 48

Find what incentives work for your child

I have a child who can be persuaded to do just about anything, if he thinks you'll be disappointed in him if he doesn't do it. It's really useful, though I do have to be careful not to emotionally blackmail him (see Rule 24). He desperately wants to please, and I can use that to motivate him. Of course, after he's done whatever it is I have to remember to tell him how pleased, impressed, delighted, touched I am with him.

I have another child who couldn't be less interested in my approval or disapproval. As far as he's concerned, that's my stuff. On the other hand, he cares very much about appearing to be grown up and being seen as responsible. So that's the lever I use to motivate him.

All my children are motivated by different things, and they're not necessarily the same things I'm motivated by (though I find chocolate works almost universally – but of course we shouldn't incentivise children with sweets, Rule 34). Some of these things are emotional incentives – approval, being seen as grown up, being appreciated. Others are more specific incentives to encourage your child to do what you want – being given more responsibility, status, money, freedom. In other words, they can be rewarded with being allowed to cook for the whole family, or allowed clothes that they think will increase their status among their friends, or given a later bedtime.

The point is that you can't just use the same old incentives on each child, because it won't work. Not only will you not get the best out of them, but they won't get whatever it is they really want. So you have to think through what incentives will work for your child, and find ways to use these. The precise rewards you offer will change as they get older, but you'll probably find that your particularly freedom-loving 2-year-old will grow up to be a particularly freedom-loving teenager. Although they may no longer be motivated by being allowed to walk upstairs without holding your hand.

Incidentally, on those rare occasions when you're looking for sticks rather than carrots, your children will respond to different threats. One may not care if you stop their pocket money for a week, while another might be devastated. It will be the same basic principles you're tapping into – freedom, money, status, approval.

So don't assume your kids are the same as each other, or the same as you. Sometimes it takes a long time to work out what the right incentive is, but if you think and experiment enough, you'll always find something.

> # YOU CAN'T JUST USE THE SAME OLD INCENTIVES ON EACH CHILD, BECAUSE IT WON'T WORK

RULE 49

Every child should have something they know they're good at

I have a cousin who has severe learning disabilities and is physic-ally poorly co-ordinated, which makes art, sport or playing an instrument very difficult. For many years it was hard to see what he was good at, quite honestly. His brother was a very talented musician and loved to listen to music, and it gradually became clear that although Dan couldn't play an instrument like his brother, he had a huge appreciation for music. If you put a tape on in the car, within two bars he would shout out the first line of the song. Yep, that's right, he was brilliant at something – he could win 'beat the intro' against anyone.

Now most kids are luckier than this – they don't have the odds so heavily stacked against them. But it shows that even the most challenged kids can still be good at something. Your child needs to know that they're good at something – beat the intro will do fine – for their self-esteem. If you want them to grow up feeling they can contribute something to the world, and hold their head up, this is their starting place. As time goes on, it will give them the confidence to find other things they're good at too. Some kids are good at loads of things, and some at only one or two that really matter to them. Your job is to keep looking until you find the thing they can excel at, and then make sure they know it.

It doesn't have to be anything academic or school-oriented (music, sport, art), although these will do fine. It might be that they've got the best memory and can remind you of all the things you've forgotten to put on the shopping list. Or maybe they're the best organizer in the family and can keep all the DVDs in order. Or perhaps they cook a mean macaroni cheese, or they have a way with animals. Just make sure they know they're good at it and – almost more important – they know that *you* know they're good at it.

By the way, this is even more important as you go down the family. The oldest is generally better than their siblings at most things for a long time. If you have several children, it's pretty difficult for the younger ones to shine (I was number five so I know what I'm talking about). So make sure the little ones manage to find their niche too.

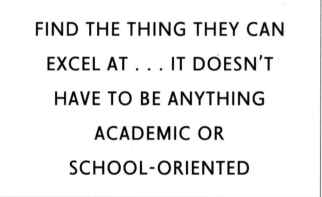

FIND THE THING THEY CAN EXCEL AT . . . IT DOESN'T HAVE TO BE ANYTHING ACADEMIC OR SCHOOL-ORIENTED

RULE 50

Learn to appreciate the qualities that remind you of someone else

When my daughter was younger, she reminded me of both her grandmothers. Now, I don't want to get personal in any way, but given a choice that's not who I'd have chosen to create (not both rolled into one, anyway). As she got older – well, she reminded me even more of her grandmothers. Of course she had some of their good points, but I didn't really notice that. It was the bad points that kept throwing themselves in front of me.

The thing is, though, she was my daughter. And I loved her unconditionally. So I learnt to love those qualities in her that had, at first, been hard to take. It's not easy to do, but it has to be done because you can't blame your kids for their genetic make-up. If anything, it made me more sympathetic to her grandmothers.

The hardest thing to learn to love is any quality that reminds you of your ex. If you're divorced or split up, your kids will constantly remind you of your ex-partner, and you have got to learn to love that side of them, even if you hate it in their other parent.

Look, I haven't got all the answers, and this one is really tough. But I can tell you what helps me. I've come to realize that there is no such thing as a bad quality; it's only how people use their natural characteristics that matters. I knew a kid who was unbelievably stubborn as a child. I mean, off the normal scale. She grew up and became an activist for good causes. You have to be unbelievably stubborn and determined to drive through important changes in the face of politicians who don't seem to care. Meanwhile she mellowed in her personal life, of course, and became a charming young woman. So is stubbornness a bad quality? Not in her case.

Just because your child reminds you of her mother or your dad or Great Auntie Betty, it doesn't mean they'll make the same use of those qualities. So there's no need to resent them. You know what you have to do: instil the values that will ensure they use their natural talents wisely.

> # THERE IS NO SUCH THING
> # AS A BAD QUALITY

Look for the similarities between you

With certain kids you can just skip on to the next Rule here. Sometimes your child reminds you of yourself constantly, and the tough thing is remembering that they don't always think the same way as you.

But some children are the opposite. You look at them wondering how they can possibly be yours. You have nothing in common and you have no clue as to how their mind works. They behave in ways that are anathema to you. Why would anyone want to burst into tears when you get cross, you wonder, instead of answer back? How can they think of playing with slugs and spiders when you don't even want to think about them?

Of course, there's no reason why you shouldn't like, admire and love this child as much as any other. But you may sometimes feel like an outside observer, and it can be hard to deal with their more emotional moments when they make no sense to you. Your child can pick up on this and there can be a sense of distance. Maybe your partner more often deals with them because they can identify with them better, but that only serves to emphasize the difference.

Now listen. I know how it feels, I've been there myself. But 50 per cent of this child's genes come from you, and there must be something in there you can recognize. You need to find it because, if you don't, your child may mistake your lack of empathy for lack of love. Especially if they have siblings, they may unconsciously realize that you seem closer to your other child or children. It can be particularly hard if you are also the opposite sex from them.

Anyone who has an adopted child will tell you how important this is. Many adoptive parents work really hard at this because they're smart enough to see that it's vital to find common ground with their kids. But some of the rest of us can feel just as different from our biological children, and we need to make the same effort to connect with them.

So keep looking until you find it. Of course children change, and sometimes a child you found it hard to identify with comes to resemble you far more as they grow up. But you can't count on that. Find shared interests, or discover that you like the same books, or ask your parents if they see any similarities. Work hard on finding time for just the two of you to be together, and see if you have similar tastes even if your personalities seem a million miles apart.

If you do all this, your child will feel equally loved and involved with you, and that's the most important thing. And the bonus is that it's often the children who are most different from you, that you learn the most from.

> ## 50 PER CENT OF THIS CHILD'S GENES COME FROM YOU AND THERE MUST BE SOMETHING IN THERE YOU CAN RECOGNIZE

Find qualities to admire in them

There's no point being alive if you're not going to keep learning. You might as well just fall off your perch now. And one of the best things about having kids is that you can learn so much from them.

It would be very boring if your kids were just like you. Where's the fun in that? Don't expect them to be like you because they won't be. And they won't like the things you do either. If you love cricket, they'll be a football fan. If you love clothes, they'll just want to hang around in dirty old jeans all the time. It's their job. They're programmed to separate themselves from you, and they'll do it increasingly as they get older, by acting differently and spending their time in different ways from you.

The way to deal with this bit of having kids is to embrace it. Instead of being sorry to see them going a different way from you, enjoy it for what you can learn. Your kids can show you things you'd never heard of, never thought about – and what a kick they get out of being able to teach you something you didn't know or couldn't do. They can teach you skills you can't get out of learning but which challenge you (talking technology here, especially). And, best of all, they can behave in ways you'd like to. Yes, your kids can effortlessly handle situations that you have always struggled with.

There is so much to admire in any kid, and your admiration will mean more to them than almost anyone's (even if they won't admit it). I have a child who can tell people openly and frankly what he thinks without caring whether they like or approve of him as a result. Now this seems perfectly natural to me but his mother, who has always been under-assertive and cursed* with a need to

---

* Her word, not mine.

be liked even by people she doesn't care for, admires him enormously for his ability to be clear and assertive. (Funnily enough, she's not quite so full of praise when I do the same thing.)

I have another child who is a supreme diplomat. Now I can just about strain to be diplomatic when I have to, but it's out of my comfort zone. He, on the other hand, is a natural and I'm often amazed at the tactics he comes up with to defuse potential squabbles. If I can't learn from him, I'll never learn, because he's the best example I know and he's right under my nose.

> ## IT WOULD BE VERY BORING IF YOUR KIDS WERE JUST LIKE YOU

RULE 53

Let them be better than you

I can remember on holiday once watching a parent on a tennis court desperately trying to beat his teenage son. The son was trying really hard to win, but the father was even more determined to hold on. Dad was red in the face, puffing and panting, but he was going to get those balls back over the net no matter what. And he did. Eventually he won and they left the court, the father looking drained but smug and the son looking resigned. I imagine he was used to it.

I felt sorry for him. The dad, I mean. The momentary satisfaction of winning just doesn't compare with the enduring satisfaction of seeing your kids' delight when they beat you. I consoled myself with the fact that it was only a matter of time. The lad was a good player and sooner or later, as he got stronger and his dad got older, his time would come.

Now, you and I know that this father clearly wasn't a Rules parent. And what I didn't tell you was that he wasn't even encouraging his son – too worried he might actually get beaten, I suppose. Of course, you can't always let your kids beat you at everything – that would be horribly patronising. You can do it when they're 2 years old, but you won't fool them when they're 12. But they can win occasionally; all you have to do is not try quite so absurdly hard as the tennis dad did. And you can encourage them even when they lose: 'Once your backhand gets as good as your forehand, I won't stand a chance.'

And if their tennis isn't quite up to yours yet, go tree-climbing with them. Or swimming. Or bake cakes together. Or play the piano. Or their favourite PlayStation game. Find something they can do better than you, and then do it together. It's so much more fun than winning (at least when it's your own kid).

And one more thing. What do you think that tennis dad taught his son about being a good loser? Nothing. Zero. Zilch. Sweet FA. All he taught him on the subject was to make sure it never happens to you. He didn't give himself a chance to demonstrate how to lose graciously. Actually, it's not so bad being a loser, so long as you're not a bad loser.

> ## IT'S NOT SO BAD BEING A LOSER, SO LONG AS YOU'RE NOT A BAD LOSER

Their attitude is as important as their achievements

What do you praise your child most for? Good schoolwork? Doing well in exams? Winning in sports? Passing grades in music?

Well done. If you're a Rules parent you spotted that was a trick question and the answer should be: none of the above. Of course it's important to congratulate your child on these things. They matter to them, so they'd be really upset if you didn't care. But the things that they deserve most praise for are to do with their attitudes and their behaviour, not their achievements.

I know a little girl who really struggles to behave well. She wants to, but she's so full of frustrations and angst that it just doesn't seem possible to be good sometimes. Unluckily for her, she has a perfectly behaved older sister. Occasionally people compare the two and comment on how much better the older one is (I'm pleased to say her parents have more sense than to do this). I feel sorry for the little girl because I can see that she tries so hard to be good. Her sister, on the other hand, isn't trying at all. So which one deserves the most praise? (Incidentally, going back to Rule 39, this is an excellent example of where carrots are so much more effective than sticks. This little girl tries so much harder when people notice she's managed to behave well.)

The things you praise or reward your child for tell them a lot about what you believe is important in life. It helps create their values. So if you always praise high achievement, academic prowess, winning, success, those are the things you tell them matter (and the pressure is on them to keep achieving). Whereas if you praise effort, perseverance, progress, diplomacy, integrity, honesty – that's what your children will grow up believing in.

Obviously you need a mix. I'm not saying you should ignore your child's achievements. I'm just saying make sure you acknowledge *all* the things that you want to matter to them, and give some thought to the balance that you strike.

> # THE THINGS YOU PRAISE OR REWARD YOUR CHILD FOR TELL THEM A LOT ABOUT WHAT YOU BELIEVE IS IMPORTANT IN LIFE

RULE 55

Keep your fears and insecurities to yourself

Here's a scenario you may recognize – I've seen it many times. You're at a zoo of some kind, and you're in the reptile section. A family is watching a beautiful snake with exquisite markings as it moves gracefully along a branch. The watching mother[*] says, 'Ugh! It's horrible!' The same often happens at the spider enclosure, and again at the scorpion tank.

Now luckily, some kids have got more sense than to take any notice of this. (And most mothers have more sense than to do it.) But there are kids who are susceptible to this, and many, many children who learn to say 'Ugh!' to reptiles and creepy crawlies because grown-ups are stupid enough to set an example. Actually these creatures are beautiful, and children should be encouraged to appreciate them, or at least to reach negative views by themselves rather than with active encouragement.

Children are heavily influenced by us, and you can saddle your kids with all sorts of worries if you're not careful. Since they're bound to come up with plenty of fears of their own, they really don't need yours as well. So keep them to yourself.

One Rules mother I know was really afraid of spiders. Bordering on the phobic. But because she didn't want her little girl to feel the same way, if there was a spider in the girl's bedroom, along would come Mum with a duster to catch the offending creature and shake it out of the window. It would leave her trembling but the little girl never knew because Mum was so determined to keep it to herself. Except for the time she dropped the spider by accident, realized what had happened, but couldn't face searching for

---

[*] I thought long and hard about whether to say this as I know it's sexist, but frankly it always is the mother.

it. So she pretended it had gone out of the window. She only got found out when the little girl pulled back the covers of her bed to get in and found the spider sitting there waiting for her. Oops.

I'm not just talking about spiders or snakes, of course. I'm talking about things like, say, fear of being abducted. Naturally you want them to develop a healthy wariness, but not an excessive fear that is disproportionate to the risks. That can be hugely and unnecessarily limiting on their social life. Or what about fear of failure? I know one father who discouraged his children from applying to university because they'd be so upset if they didn't get in.

It can be hard to bite your tongue, and your kids will pick up on hidden signals too, but the more you try to conceal your personal worries, the better chance you have of succeeding. That frees your children up to enjoy life and make their own discoveries – and develop their very own insecurities without any help from you.

SINCE THEY'RE BOUND
TO COME UP WITH PLENTY
OF FEARS OF THEIR OWN,
THEY REALLY DON'T NEED
YOURS AS WELL

Mind your programming

I was at school with a kid whose dad went prematurely grey at the age of 30. He was hugely embarrassed by this for some reason, and kept going on about how awful it was being grey at such an early age. Guess what happened? Yep, his son went grey at 30 too. And having spent his whole childhood being told how embarrassing and awful this was, he naturally felt embarrassed and awful about it. His father tried to reassure him but of course it rang hollow – you can't spend 25 years telling someone that a thing is awful and then suddenly change your mind and expect them to follow suit.

What don't you like about yourself? Are you fat (in your view)? Bald? Have a funny nose? Weird knees? A stammer? If so, please keep it to yourself. If you don't mention it, your kids will have no reason to form a negative view of it. And they may inherit it from you. Whatever you say about yourself now, they'll hear echoing in their ears in 20 or 30 years' time.

Just suppose my friend's dad had worn his grey hair with pride (or at least pretended to)? Suppose he'd joked to his son, 'I think it makes me look rather distinguished, don't you?' My friend would have had a totally different self-image when he went grey.

We shouldn't criticise each other in front of the kids (or, indeed, out of their hearing), but obviously the same thing applies. Don't tease your partner for wearing glasses, or call them 'baldy', however affectionately, or criticise them for putting on weight. You are programming your kids subliminally and you won't discover the damage you've done until it's too late. They're not going to be convinced when you change your tune in 30 years' time: 'Oh, darling, I didn't mean *you*. You look much better bald than I do.'

If you know your kids are likely to inherit a particular trait, you would do better to put a positive spin on it in front of them. Tell your partner how clever they look in their glasses, or mention the advantages of being a tall woman rather than the disadvantages. You never know, you might even start to convince yourself too.

> WHATEVER YOU SAY ABOUT YOURSELF NOW, THEY'LL HEAR ECHOING IN THEIR EARS IN 20 OR 30 YEARS' TIME

RULE 57

Don't try to have a perfect child

Rule 2 was about you not being perfect. Well, now it's your child's turn. If you try to bring up your child to be perfect you will, quite obviously, fail. You'll also put them under unfair pressure and, as we Rules parents have worked out by now, it's all too easy to pressurise our children and it's a Bad Thing.

In any case, who wants a perfect child? In fact, more to the point, what is a perfect child? I can't imagine such a thing. Every child I've ever met who was impeccably behaved and never put a foot wrong, strove to please their parents and their teachers, worked hard at school and always handed in their homework on time, was the most boring characterless little prig imaginable.

All the kids I've liked the most, who have had the biggest and warmest personalities, have been wonderfully flawed. They've all had an overly mischievous tendency, or a temper when riled, or a sense of humour that sometimes went too far, or a lazy streak (that they generally made up for with charm). I've known countless fabulous kids over the years, who have grown up into terrific adults, but I couldn't say, hand on heart, that any of them was perfect. Thank goodness.

Children aren't supposed to be mini grown-ups. They're meant still to have all those imperfections that growing up is intended to eradicate. If you had them perfect by the age of 10 you might as well send them off then to be merchant bankers. You'd have defeated the purpose of the next few years. Childhood is for being a child and, privately, I always think kids turn out best if not quite all those early imperfections disappear. Who wants an adult child who never has a mischievous twinkle in their eye, or a hint of impetuosity, or a daft sense of humour, or a bit of wild adventurousness left in them?

The only kind of child it's worth aiming to raise is a child who is able to indulge their own individual personality with self-assurance, and has the understanding not to hurt other people in the process. That's as good as it gets. And that covers an awful lot of kids, I'm pleased to say. And I'm sure none of them is perfect.

> ## ALL THE KIDS I'VE LIKED THE MOST, WHO HAVE HAD THE BIGGEST AND WARMEST PERSONALITIES, HAVE BEEN WONDERFULLY FLAWED

SIBLING RULES

If you have more than one child, you'll have worked out for yourself that there's a whole new dynamic going on that needs its own set of rules. I know a headmaster of a boys' school who was asked by a local farmer, many decades ago now, if he could lend him one of his students to help with some farm work. The headmaster said he was sure he could find more than one willing helper if needed. The farmer declined saying, 'One boy's a boy, two boys is half a boy, and three boys is no boy at all'.

No doubt he'd have said much the same about girls. The fact is the more children you put together, the harder it becomes to keep them all on track. Not just because of the numbers, but because of the interactions between them. So this section is about the most important Rules you need to get you through when you have two or more children. It goes without saying that these Rules apply as much to step-siblings as to any others.

RULE 58

Give them each other

I think this is the most important sibling Rule of all, and it's the guiding Rule for all the others. So listen closely. The most important thing you can ever do for your children is give them the best possible relationships with each other.

There are plenty of ways of bringing up siblings, from deliberately dividing them right through to consciously bonding them together. And if you aim for the latter, your children will be each other's very closest friends for life. And, once they're adults, they will need equal siblings as much as they need parents who are, inevitably, not equals (not that we're superior, but the relationship isn't, and shouldn't be, balanced; see Rule 102 before you start arguing with me). And what's more, in all probability and hope, their siblings will be around for them long after you've gone.

I know families who are widely spread around the globe, but when one of them is in trouble, it's their siblings, continents away, they know they can count on. If that's what you want for your kids (and as a Rules parent of course it is), the preparation starts now.

There are lots of ways you can help bond your children together. For a start, you can refuse to countenance tale-telling ('She may have left the tap running, but you shouldn't be telling tales on your sister. That's not a kind thing to do'). That sends out a clear message that you value their goodwill towards each other.

Then you can encourage them to help each other: 'I'm not very good at maths, but I'm sure Sam can help with your homework.' If they behave well, you can reward them collectively – everyone gets a shared treat for cooking lunch together, or making sure the dog got walked every day this week. Talk to them all together, at meal times or in the car, to tell them what's going on: 'Granny and Grandpa are coming to stay this weekend . . . .' And as they get older, involve them all in group decisions about where to go on holiday, or what colour to repaint the bathroom. It's important as well that you do your best to remove any scope for rivalry or jealousy between your kids. There's plenty more about this later on, especially in Rule 63.

Here's another thing that's guaranteed to bring any group of people together, siblings or not: let them unite against a common enemy. What enemy? Why you, of course. Nothing bonds siblings faster than being able to have a good moan about their parents. All petty internal feuding will be forgotten, and they'll be in total agreement with each other. So next time you make a decision that they all hate, just remember that you're helping to forge crucial bonds between them for life.

> **NOTHING BONDS SIBLINGS FASTER THAN BEING ABLE TO HAVE A GOOD MOAN ABOUT THEIR PARENTS**

RULE 59

Recognize that squabbling is healthy (within reason)

If you have more than one child – and unless you started with twins you can't say you didn't know better – you'll be no stranger to the sound of squabbling. Some do it more than others, but they all do it. And half the frustration is that it's usually just so pointless. Or is it?

Does it really matter who that computer game actually belongs to? Or who's got the coolest shoes? Or who goes out through the front door first (yes, mine have actually squabbled ferociously about this)? Well, the short answer obviously is no. Not to you anyway.

But it does matter that our children learn how to squabble. Why? Because until they know how to squabble properly, they can't learn how *not* to squabble. And we really want them to grow up able to not squabble. Have you noticed how children without siblings (you may have been one yourself) often find conflict more difficult to cope with as adults? They have to fight a tendency to be too aggressive or, at the other extreme, too under-assertive, whereas most of the natural diplomats I've encountered in life grew up with siblings.

The only way to learn diplomacy, compromise and all those related skills that young children (and far too many adults) aren't too good at, is to squabble. Squabbling teaches you how you can and can't get other people to co-operate with you. Over the years children learn that their brother becomes less accommodating if you punch him in the face, or that their sister won't let you in her room unless you allow her into yours. It's much harder for them to find these things out by practising on their friends, because it's a pretty good way of ending up with no friends. Siblings, on the other hand, can't say 'I won't be your brother if you don't play with me'. They are endlessly forgiving, if only because they have no choice.

Sibling squabbles are often power struggles. They establish the pecking order (status), or whose space is whose (territory), or who is allowed to make their own decisions (independence). You have to adopt a policy of non-intervention in these basic issues (even if you send in a peace-keeping force when violence breaks out), because you can't change your children's inherent characters by trying to make it fair. Look at the Balkans, the Middle East, Vietnam – it simply doesn't work when you try to make their choices for them. And, boy, can your kids seem to be as much trouble as warring nations at times.

So next time your children squabble (shouldn't be too long to wait), appreciate it. Oh OK, that's asking a bit much, but at least don't imagine you've gone wrong somewhere, or that you should be stopping them from squabbling. Because, actually, they're not so much squabbling as learning essential skills for life.

> **SQUABBLING TEACHES YOU HOW YOU CAN AND CAN'T GET OTHER PEOPLE TO CO-OPERATE WITH YOU**

RULE 60

Teach them to sort out their own arguments

You had an easy time of it with the last Rule. Nothing to do but sit back and relax. This one is a bit more difficult, but it's an essential follow-on to Rule 59.

Once you accept that squabbling is a necessary evil – part of learning to compromise and co-operate – you also have to accept that it won't work unless you leave the kids to get on with it. Otherwise they've learnt nothing, except that if they shout loud enough, or hit hard enough, a grown-up will come and sort it out for them. They're going to be very disappointed when they leave home and no grown-up magically appears to settle all their disputes.

Sadly, a lot of children do grow up like this. I went on a training course many years ago where a group of managers was asked to build a tower out of odd-shaped bricks. It was quite scary how quickly it descended into a shouting match. Ironic, really, given that the idea was to find out how well we could co-operate. It didn't matter a monkey's whether the tower stayed up or not.

Nope, there's nothing for it: if you want your kids to grow up able to succeed in training exercises, not to mention life in general, you're going to have to bite your tongue and put up with the noise and squabbles. And funnily enough, when you do that, it doesn't take that long before most of the squabbles get resolved without you.

Of course, we all have days when we just haven't the patience or the time to wait for the children to sort it out among themselves. In that case you can get creative about intervening without letting them off finding a solution themselves. For example, you can take away the toy they're fighting over, or turn off the computer or TV, and tell them, 'You can have it back when you can both (or all) agree to a solution'.

I know one couple who use a great trick with their children. It works particularly well for them as they have all boys (they're so competitive). They hold what they call an 'honesty competition'. This one's good for those fights where you can't hope to get to the bottom of who started it. You say, 'We'll have a competition to see who can be the most honest'. (See, this is where the boys fall for it every time.) Then you ask each in turn, 'What did you do that you shouldn't have done?' The rule is they can't refer to anything the other one (allegedly) did. I've known this couple's children confess to all sorts of things, and ask for a further 137 offences to be taken into consideration, just for the chance to win the honesty competition. At the end of the confession you ask them each to apologize for the things they've admitted to, and then send them on their way. It helps them understand that it takes two to squabble – and it doesn't half make you feel good too.

> **ONCE YOU ACCEPT THAT SQUABBLING IS NECESSARY, YOU ALSO HAVE TO ACCEPT THAT IT WON'T WORK UNLESS YOU LEAVE THE KIDS TO GET ON WITH IT**

Work as a team

This isn't just about you and your partner, although obviously you do need to work as a team. But this is the siblings section of the book, so this Rule is about getting the whole family to work as a team. It's all part of giving your kids a great relationship with each other.

Working as a team might mean all mucking in together, or it might mean each doing individual jobs that together get the whole thing done. It doesn't matter which you're doing, so long as the kids know it's a team effort.

We have a rule in our house that at the end of a meal, everyone has to help tidy up until the kitchen is clear. Then everyone can stop. The kids are very used to this and they muck in together. One will load the dishwasher while another puts the butter away or puts any leftovers in the compost or the dog's bowl. Being a shared chore (grown-ups aren't excused) means that the faster each of them works, the more everyone gains, and they can see this. Often one will say to another, 'Here, I'll take that off you while you stack the dishes', because they can see it's in their own interests too.

There are lots of chances to exploit this kind of teamwork. You could, of course, get the kids to take turns clearing the kitchen, but you'd be missing an opportunity for them to work as a team.

We learnt another good team exercise from some friends of ours. When they go to the beach for the day, the kids help assemble everything to take with them. One gets the towels, another the surfboards, another sorts out a picnic lunch. They're all doing separate jobs, but they're aware that they're all pulling in the same direction, i.e. getting to the beach as soon as possible.

Crises are the best opportunities of all for team building, and the more fun you can make it, the better. When I was young, we had a drain that used to flood about once every year or two when there was heavy rain, and it threatened to engulf the garage (where we kept various things that mustn't get wet, like the freezer). As soon as we realized it was happening, we all used to pile out in the rain, often in pyjamas with coats and wellies over the top, with brooms to sweep the water away from the garage, while someone cleared all the dead leaves out of the drain. We all worked together for about half an hour getting it clear, usually having a good laugh as we did it, and then collapsed back indoors to hot chocolate and, although we were far too unsentimental to admit it, actually a rather good sense of team spirit.

CRISES ARE THE BEST OPPORTUNITIES OF ALL FOR TEAM BUILDING

RULE 62

Let them entertain each other

Any parent with only one child will know that it can be very hard work. You have to be their entertainer, best friend and playmate as well as their parent because, most of the time, there's no one else to do those jobs.

Once you have more than one child, however, they can perform those roles for each other, leaving you free to get on with being their parent (and, hopefully, putting your feet up with the paper occasionally). You are not copping out when you do this. Quite the reverse.

It's much better for your children to entertain each other than for you to entertain them all the time. Of course that doesn't mean you're never allowed to play with them, but it's very rarely as equal as we think. Generally you'll be coming up with more ideas than them, or at least guiding their ideas. And if you don't do that, you're letting them have their own way without learning to compromise. You can't win, see.

Siblings, on the other hand, can play together equally. Sure, one of them may be the dominant of the two while the other gives in most often (the more siblings there are, the more complicated the interactions become), but you have to leave that to them. You can't change their inherent character, and you'll probably find that when they're finally grown up, the one that always backed down will be the better diplomat and team player. So don't be tempted to interfere to redress the balance. It's their stuff, and they'll sort it out their way, squabbles and all.

Some parents have one child who wants to play with their sibling, while the sibling likes to be left alone. Short of having another child just to solve the problem (which it will, if the gap's not too big), this is still something you have to let them sort out among themselves. They'll end up compromising – your loner will become a bit more gregarious, and your socialite will learn to amuse themselves. That can't be a bad thing now, can it?

So don't feel guilty about that cup of tea and a paper with your feet up,* because you're doing the best thing for your kids by butting out and leaving them to entertain each other.

> # IT'S THEIR STUFF, AND THEY'LL SORT IT OUT THEIR WAY, SQUABBLES AND ALL

---

* I know, I know, there's a pile of washing before you can have a cup of tea, and the kitchen to tidy, and the vacuuming, and a meal to cook . . .

RULE 63

Never compare children with each other

I know a couple who have two children – one (as so often) is predominantly very well behaved, and the other is frequently naughty. And to some extent it's the parents' own fault. Why? Because they actually say to the naughty one,* 'Why can't you behave as nicely as your sister?' If that isn't a red rag to a bull, I don't know what is.

There's no way your children are going to have an easy relationship if jealousies and rivalries are allowed to grow up between them. So don't ever let one of them know that you think they're better at sport than the others, or not as clever, or funny, or talented. No, that doesn't mean you have to pretend that they're equally good at everything. That would be silly. But you don't have to point out inequalities that they might not have thought about, and you don't have to comment on any of their abilities *in relation to each other.*

That's the critical thing. You can tell your child, 'You're really talented at art', without telling them, 'You're better than your brother at art'. After all, why pick on their poor brother? It's no more relevant than the fact that they're better than Fred Bloggs at art, is it? But it gives the impression that you view your children as a co-ordinating set rather than as individuals. And in this case it tells their poor brother that he's the shop-soiled one of the set.

We'll see in Rule 67 that it can be a good thing to let your kids know what they're good at. All I'm saying is that you should treat their talents and their shortcomings in isolation from their siblings. After all, it doesn't actually matter whether they can cook,

---

* Yes, well spotted, I just broke Rule 42. But the kid wasn't listening.

sing, trampoline, add up, take phone messages, speak French, tell jokes, brush their hair or anything else, better or worse than each other. All that matters is that they can do it.

Of course, your kids may not see it like this. Boys are typically the most competitive, but often girls can give them a run for their money too. Odds are your children will pester you with questions along the lines of, 'My drawing's better than hers, isn't it?' or 'I can run faster than him, can't I?' So what you gonna say?

The answer is to do what you always promised yourself as a child that you'd never do when you were a grown-up, and duck the issue. You can say, 'It's hard to judge. You've drawn those trees beautifully. The detail in the leaves is wonderful. She's used lovely colours, though, and her colouring-in is getting very good'. Or, 'You should be able to run faster – you're two years older'.

> # THERE'S NO WAY YOUR CHILDREN ARE GOING TO HAVE AN EASY RELATIONSHIP IF JEALOUSIES AND RIVALRIES ARE ALLOWED TO GROW UP BETWEEN THEM

RULE 64

Different children need different rules

Broadly speaking, I don't consider this book controversial. That's not my aim – I'm just trying to flag up some key principles, most of which are common sense but that are easier to follow once they've been put into words, and which maybe you hadn't consciously thought about too much before. As I said at the beginning of the book – it's not a revelation. It's a reminder. But I suspect that if anyone wants to argue with me, this is the Rule they'd pick to dispute. It appears to contradict Rules 31, 40, 61 and probably several others we haven't got to yet. But it only *appears* to.

Rule 13 was about adapting your expectations of your children to the reality of their individual character. This Rule goes one step further – sometimes you do actually have to have different rules for each of your children.

Your children are not the same as each other and it therefore stands to reason that a one-size-fits-all approach to rules simply can't be right. Of course your children won't appreciate this when they think they're on the wrong end of things, so some rules must apply to everyone. Call them house rules if you like. It's only fair that everyone has to go to bed when they're asked to, or clear up after meals. But other rules will have to be adapted to your child's personality.

I'll be honest with you. When I first started out as a parent, I thought it was unfair to bend rules for one child and not another. It seemed obvious to me that you had to have the same rules for everyone. And then my children started to grow. And I realized that certain rules were asking far more of one child than another.

Here's an example. I have one son who is pathologically untidy. He is messy on an industrial scale.* He has no idea that he is,

---

* Yep, there goes Rule 42 again. But I'm not saying which son.

because he has a strange condition that renders him unable to see the chaos he leaves around him. Asking him to tidy up after himself is simply not the same as asking his siblings to tidy up. We'd be demanding 20 times as much of him because (a) he can't see the mess, (b) he doesn't understand why it's a problem anyway (it's not bothering him), and (c) it would take him several hours a day. So actually, applying the same rule to all of them would be hugely unfair on him.

Of course, we don't let him off the hook. But we do settle for less than the others. He has to do some tidying, and we help so long as he's genuinely working at it too. As he gets older, so the onus gradually passes to him.

This son, I should say, has a very good attention span, and is expected to sit down and work at his homework for a good half hour at a stretch, which he does with no problem. One of his (tidy) siblings, however, finds it really hard to work in more than 10-minute bursts, so he's allowed to spread his homework over a whole weekend in shorter sessions.

In other words, sometimes the same rules for everyone is the only fair approach, but there are times when it can be unfair, and you have to look out for these. The important thing is how much you're asking of each child.

> # THE IMPORTANT THING IS HOW MUCH YOU'RE ASKING OF EACH CHILD

Don't have a favourite

Admitting to having a favourite child is actually one of the great taboos. Lots of people will simply tell you, 'You mustn't have a favourite'. Well, I'm sure that would be lovely, but maybe you can't help it. Some parents really have no trouble with this one. They just aren't made that way and they couldn't have a favourite if they tried. Others, however, simply can't help preferring one child to another, and if they said they didn't have a favourite, they'd be lying.

If this is the case, lying is unquestionably the answer. Under no circumstances should you ever reveal who is your favourite child to anyone, except possibly your partner. And to avoid revealing it, you may have to lie and claim you have no favourite. I can remember my grandmother once telling me that I was my aunt's favourite nephew. Of course I glowed, but she was completely out of order telling me. You see, you can't rely on people not to say something in a moment of aberration.

I know one parent who tells me that he does have a favourite child – he can't help it – but that it isn't always the same one. All of his children have been favourites at certain times, and all still take turns in the role without knowing it. He also tells me that, actually, he has always loved them equally. It's just that he often likes one best.

So what can you do if you have a favourite (apart from lie about it)? Well, for a start you can consider whether you really love one best, or whether in fact you simply like them best. Perhaps it's just that you feel closest to them, which isn't the same thing as loving them most. It may be that you do love your children equally really, and you just can't see it.

That will work for some people, but not everyone. If you still feel you really love one best, you need to work on your relationship with the other. Look for the lovable qualities in them consciously, maybe spend more time with them, or find a common interest and take time to do it together – trains, fishing, clothes shopping, horror movies (talking older kids here obviously), walking, food, horses, football, whatever.

By the way, your children are always on the lookout for any clue as to which of them is your favourite. They may well ask you directly, and even if they don't they'll pick up the slightest hint, often wilfully misinterpreting you in order to elicit this prized information. Generally speaking, if they all accuse you of differing preferences, you're probably doing fine. If they all think you have the same favourite – whether they're right or wrong – that's when you need to worry about the signals you're giving them.

UNDER NO CIRCUMSTANCES SHOULD YOU EVER REVEAL WHO IS YOUR FAVOURITE CHILD TO ANYONE

Mix and match

This Rule helps to build your relationships with your kids, and their relationships with each other. It also helps things along if you're in any danger of having a favourite child, resenting certain qualities in your children, or feeling you don't have enough in common with them.

Lots of traditional families (especially two parents + two kids families) tend to hang out together a lot. Maybe during the week one or other of the parents will be off working, but at weekends they all go out as a family. I know loads of families like this, and it's generally reckoned to be a good thing.

Well, yes . . . and no. You can have too much of a good thing. It's important to make sure that you also spend time in as many different combinations and permutations as you can:

- Make sure each child gets time alone with each parent.

- Both/all kids hang out with one of the parents (vary which one).

- One child can have both parents to themselves while the other(s) are elsewhere.

- For families with three or more children, two kids can spend time with one parent while the other(s) go with parent number two. Don't always split this the same way.

This also gives you the opportunity to develop special relationships with each child. Maybe child 1 gets to cook with one parent and go for walks with the other. Meantime child 2 looks at books with one and plays in the park with the other. If each child has their own special thing that they alone do with each parent, they will all get to feel really special.

It's an especially valuable system if your family includes stepchildren or half-siblings. This approach gives everyone the chance to forge individual relationships with each other, rather than only seeing their step-parent, for example, when the step-brothers and sisters are there too.

If you're a single parent, of course this is much harder.* But it's still worth taking every opportunity to have someone else look after one or more of the kids while you get time with the others. And when you can get one child to yourself – maybe the others are with friends or at a party – do something special with them, rather than just getting the housework done with less background squabbling.

MAKE SURE THAT YOU SPEND
TIME IN AS MANY DIFFERENT
COMBINATIONS AND
PERMUTATIONS AS
YOU CAN

---

* Or if you have 12 kids, I imagine. But if that's the case you won't have found time to read this book.

RULE 67

Find each child's strengths

Rule 49 was about making sure your child knows they're good at something. That's essential, and especially so when you have more than one child. One thing you can guarantee is that they'll have very different strengths.

Gifts and talents often run in families. It may well be that if one of your kids is musically talented, or hugely athletic, or deeply artistic, or brilliantly academic, so are their siblings. Even so, it can be tough being a bassoonist whose older sister is a more advanced bassoonist. Maybe your younger child would feel they could succeed better as a cellist or a flautist. You need to encourage these small differences so that everyone can shine.

When it comes to personality, however, that's where the big differences show. Despite their genes, siblings can have wildly different strengths, and you need to encourage these (without ignoring Rule 63, Never compare children with each other). As they get older, your children will need to develop apart from each other in order to find their own individuality. They don't want to grow up to be a carbon copy of their brothers and sisters, they want to be themselves. You can help them by encouraging each to have their own strengths.

This is especially true for younger siblings, who often struggle for years to be better at anything than their older siblings. However, it's much easier for them to have character strengths than skill strengths. In other words, it's easier to be the bravest when you're aged 3 than to be the best at spelling. So – without comparing them to each other – make sure your 3-year-old knows that they're really good at being brave, or kind, or at remembering things (one of mine used to remember my mental shopping list for me at 3 years old, so long as it wasn't too long – he just had a great memory for that kind of thing).

Your child's confidence, and their sense of having a role in the family, is hugely dependent on knowing that they have real strengths within the team. So as a Rules parent, you need to find out what their strengths are, and especially those strengths which benefit the whole family – skilful navigating on long journeys, great cooking, making everyone laugh when things are going badly, solving logistical problems, smoothing over disputes, staying calm in a crisis, being able to follow technical instructions (I'm always grateful for that one, being incapable of reading instructions myself).

Just one rider here: make sure you don't always pick on someone as being 'the family navigator/cook/problem solver' if there's another child who would like the role. If you think you're a good navigator but your brother always gets asked and no one gives you the chance to show you can do it too, that can be pretty demoralising. So check no one else is being routinely and unwillingly overlooked.

> # YOUR CHILD'S CONFIDENCE IS HUGELY DEPENDENT ON KNOWING THAT THEY HAVE REAL STRENGTHS WITHIN THE TEAM

SCHOOL RULES

Love it or hate it, your child has to have some kind of schooling. And although they're not with you when they're at school (unless you are home educating of course), your attitude will make a huge difference to how well they succeed at school – and I don't just mean academically.

Your child will spend more hours at school than with you during term time, at least while they're awake (assuming they stay awake at school). So this part of their life is hugely important to them and they need to feel that you're interested, concerned and involved in it, albeit at a distance.

From when they're aged 4 or 5, right through until they're 16 or 18, there are certain basic Rules that will get you, and them, through their school career more happily.

Schooling isn't the same as education

I've known people leave school at 16 or 18 and know nothing – except perhaps their times tables and where Burkina Faso is and what the repeal of the corn laws was all about (beats me). In other words, information. That's what school gives you: information. OK, and a few analytical skills such as long division and grammar, much of which you may never use again. Some of it is useful, such as foreign languages, but much of it apparently has no value at all.

Don't get me wrong, I'm not knocking school. It teaches you how to learn – which is a useful skill for the rest of your life – but it takes 10 or 12 years or more to do it. And think about all the things it *doesn't* teach your kids during those formative years. How to think for themselves, how to change a light bulb, how to be assertive, how to stay out of debt, how to tell when a fight's brewing, how to resolve arguments amicably, how to treat people with respect, what to do when the car breaks down, how to face your fears, how to be a good loser, how to be a good winner . . .

'But school does teach you how to win and lose', I hear you say. 'What's sports day all about?' Yes, I know school gives you lots of practice at some of these things (and none at others), but they don't teach you how to do it well. They let you keep losing badly every time if you're so inclined. In any case, the things your kids get lots of practice at in school are all things they could practise just as well outside school. Because it's being in a group of kids that teaches them what behaviour is and isn't socially acceptable. The teachers have nothing to do with it. They can learn that just as well in any group of kids – in a local youth group, or football club, or down at the rec.

The point of all this is that schooling your child is not at all the same thing as educating them. Schooling is important, but not half so important as a good education. It's the school's job to school them (the clue's in the name) but it's your job to educate them. Don't expect the school to do it for you.

I know kids who have been home educated and ended up much more capable, rounded and mature people than children who've been through full-time schooling. Which rather demonstrates that school isn't necessary for a good education. I'm not telling you to home educate your child (unless you want to). I'm just saying you shouldn't rely on the school to give your child anything useful except information, and the odd practical skill such as how to play the recorder or dissect a frog. The rest is down to you.

THAT'S WHAT SCHOOL GIVES YOU: INFORMATION

School comes as a package

There's no such thing as a perfect school. Your kids' school has several hundred, even thousand, parents, and there's no way they will all agree with everything the school does. If every policy had to be agreed by a unanimous decision of all parents, they'd never even be able to agree what time to start in the mornings.

So of course you're going to disagree with things. The amount of homework the school gives them, the severity – or lack of it – of the punishments, the stupid uniform they have to wear, the fact that they make them play football even if they hate it, the fact their assemblies are secular, the fact their assemblies *aren't* secular, making pupils learn Spanish instead of German, forcing them to play indoors whenever it rains . . . and on and on and on.

There's nothing you can do about it. OK, you can change schools but the next one will have just as many irritating little ways. They'll just be different ones. And what's more, there's nothing your child can do about it. Which means that you're just going to make their school life miserable if you encourage them to undermine the system. They'll be in trouble with the teachers and quite possibly made fun of by their fellow pupils. No, they really don't need conflicting messages from home and school.

The thing to grasp about any school is that it comes as a package. There are things you like about it and things you don't. If the ones you dislike outweight the pluses, maybe you need to think about changing schools – that's another issue. But as long as you're there, you have to buy into the package as a whole. And that means that you have to support the school, even over the things you don't care for. You have to encourage your child to do their homework, even if you do think they have too much of it. And you have to get them to wear that silly uniform, or play hockey, or treat the teachers with respect even if they don't respect them.

You may be wondering what you're supposed to do if your child challenges you directly: 'Do you think it's fair to give us this much homework?' Are you supposed to lie to them? Well, you can tell them exactly what I've just told you: it's a package deal, and as long as you're there you buy into the package. That way you're educating them (see Rule 68) about how to function as part of a social group. Co-operating with the system is more important than agreeing with it.

And if you want to argue with me, please read the next Rule before you start writing in.

YOU HAVE TO BUY INTO THE PACKAGE AS A WHOLE

RULE 70

Fight your child's corner

Rule 69 was all about backing the school up, even when you don't agree with everything they do. But that doesn't have to be unconditional. You have to back them up over the policies and systems in general because that's part of the deal. But other things can crop up which are specific to your child, and you can't always leave the school to deal with it.

Your child needs to know that you're on their side. And when there are serious problems you're the only one to champion their cause – and sometimes they need a champion. If the school is not doing enough about bullying, or they're failing to recognize your child's dyslexia, or one particular teacher is making your child's life miserable, of course you need to do something about it. And your child needs to know that you're there for them if things get beyond their control. That's what parents are for. The alternative is that your child sees you allowing them to go on suffering.

It can be hard sometimes as an adult to remember the feeling of powerlessness you have as a child. Situations we can cope with easily now were impossibly daunting when we were young. And putting up with something for a few months may seem bearable now, but when you're aged 5 or even 15 a few months can seem to stretch out ahead of you forever. I can remember that sick feeling I used to get (repeatedly) before a lesson when I was going to have to fess up that I hadn't done my homework (again). If you stood me in front of that same teacher today and he tried to tear me off a strip, I'd give as good as I got. But I couldn't back then. Children are conditioned to accept the teacher's authority, and they really don't have the skills or the clout to fight the system for themselves. That's when you step in.

I'm wondering whether I should have used the word 'fight' in this Rule. Because actually, of course, diplomacy is always a better approach than belligerence, and I'm not advocating that you storm into the head's office making furious demands. It's always more effective to let them know you can see things from their viewpoint, and then guide them round to your way of thinking. This is where being a Rules parent really comes into its own. Because, as a Rules parent, you know that you need to handle the situation carefully to ensure you don't get the head's back up before you've even started.

It's worth pointing out that Rule 70 works much better if you follow Rule 69. In other words, if the school thinks of you as a parent who doesn't normally complain, they'll take you more seriously when you're unhappy. If you've moaned and criticized all through your child's school career to date, you'll have been marked down as one of *those* parents, and the school is far less likely to listen to you when something really important crops up.

> ## YOUR CHILD NEEDS TO KNOW THAT YOU'RE THERE FOR THEM IF THINGS GET BEYOND THEIR CONTROL

RULE 71

Bullying is always serious

I know a child called Ned who hates his name because it rhymes with too many things and his classmates have, obviously, spotted this, 'Ned, Ned, wets the bed' being one of their favourite chants.* Now, on one (rather pathetic) level that's quite funny of course, but Ned doesn't think so.

It's very easy for parents to brush this sort of thing off. They tell their child, 'Sticks and stones can break your bones but words can never hurt you'. Rules parents, of course, know better than that. Of course a little gentle teasing is preferable to being beaten up daily for your lunch money (which is the level of aggression we'll look at in the next Rule). But not all verbal taunts come under the category of gentle teasing. They can be very deeply hurtful and harmful to children.

The only thing that matters is how your child feels. It doesn't matter whether one child is calling them names or the whole class has sent them to Coventry. It doesn't matter whether one kid kicked them in the shins yesterday or a gang is beating up on them regularly. It doesn't matter whether you personally choose to term it teasing or taunting or bullying. The only way you can judge the severity of the problem is by how strongly your child feels about it.

And if your child is hurt and upset, you have to do something. You want to do something, of course. So do it. Depending on the circumstances, you may want to discuss with your child how they

---

* Of course, I'm sure they'd find equivalent rhymes if his name were Joe or Harry or Tom. Though maybe not Erasmus or Quauhtli. Then again, they have a far greater cross to bear.

can handle it (see Rule 72), or you may want to talk to the school. Or you may have another trick up your sleeve (changing Ned's name by deed poll might be a bit drastic). But you must let your child see that if they take it seriously, so do you.

I would sound a note of caution against approaching the other parents direct. If you were told your child was bullying other kids, you'd be pretty quick to leap to their defence, at least publicly, whatever you might say to them in private. Most encounters between parents in this situation end in anger and more deeply entrenched positions. So don't try it unless you're very sure it will make things better and not worse.

> ## YOU MUST LET YOUR CHILD SEE THAT IF THEY TAKE IT SERIOUSLY, SO DO YOU

Teach them to stand up for themselves

No, I'm not suggesting you should tell your child to punch anyone in the face who gives them a hard time. But bullying is a part of human nature and it happens in all schools (though some deal with it better than others) so you need to be prepared for it. If your child is being bullied, we've already seen that you have to do something about it. I'm here to talk Rules and I haven't got room for a whole book on dealing with bullying, but that may well be what you need.*

So what's this Rule about? Well, if your child is facing – or might ever face – bullying, the most crucial thing you can do is to teach them to handle it before it goes too far. Do you know why kids get bullied? For being different. And researchers have found that 75 per cent of kids have been upset by teasing or bullying about their appearance. In fact, one in five have skived off, played hooky, pulled a sickie to avoid being taunted about the way they look. Pretty scary figures, huh?

The two traditional methods of handling bullies are at opposite extremes. One school of thought says you should tell your child to hit back. However, not surprisingly, although this can work, it more often leads to an escalation of the problem. The other popular advice is to ignore it and the bully will stop. This is a piece of advice that some parents give because they want it to be true. But it isn't. All the evidence shows that the reverse is actually true.

So what's the answer? Your child's best bet is to look confident, make eye contact, and distract the bully by changing the subject. Of course it doesn't work in every scenario, but if your child is naturally

---

* I can thoroughly recommend *Help! I'm Being Bullied* by Dr Emily Lovegrove (Accent Press, 2006), which is written for both you and your child to read.

confident, has good self-esteem and cares about their appearance, they're halfway to not being bullied in the first place. And you can give them all those things well before they meet their first bully.

I'm not saying it's your fault – or theirs – if they get bullied. And it's not their fault if they wear glasses or have a disability. But I do know kids who wear glasses and have disabilities or disfigurements who never get bullied. This is about not giving other kids ammunition to single your child out. Of course, the occasional rather too cursory hairbrushing won't be noticed, but routine scruffiness or smelliness or tangled hair will. I was at school with a kid known universally as 'Smelly Denton'. Can't even remember what his first name was. But I can remember how he smelt, and the excuse it gave everyone to pick on him.

You can help prevent your child being bullied by making sure that they are:

- confident and self-assured

- not overweight

- well presented (washed and tidy, with clean nails, hair brushed and the like).

It's a huge start and if, on top of that, you let them know about the importance of eye contact and not looking intimidated, you'll know you've done every thing you can to protect them before trouble starts.

IT'S NOT YOUR FAULT – OR THEIRS – IF THEY GET BULLIED

Put up with friends of theirs you don't like

Have your children got any friends you're not keen on? That wild one in nursery who pulls other kids' hair when no one's looking? The girl in Year 5 who's their best friend one day and not speaking to them the next? The 15-year-old who's always playing truant (and you're quite sure he smokes)?

Yep, right through your child's school career there will be friends you wish they didn't have. Maybe you feel they upset your child, or they're a 'bad influence', luring them into cheeking the teachers or bunking off games. My mother hated any friends who didn't talk 'properly' (bit of a problem in the south London school she sent me to). Still, at least she never found out about the one who taught me to make homemade explosives in his garden shed.

So what can you do about it? Well, assuming you've read the title of this Rule you know what I'm going to say. That's right – you can just put up with it. Your child has got to learn how to pick friends for themselves, even if you don't like their choices. They have to decide for themselves when they've had enough of Kirstie playing hot and cold with their friendship. Or whether skiving off with Jake during French is really a good idea.

Ultimately, their decisions will come down to the values you've managed to impart. It takes time – they have to experiment with the wrong friends in order to recognize the right ones. So don't beat yourself up if they're hanging out with a wild crowd at the age of 6. In the end your good parenting will show through.

In the meantime, they're learning loads from their friends, whether it's good or bad. Flunking your French exams because you never turned up to lessons actually teaches you a lot more than turning up regularly and passing the exams.[*] Bad friends teach your kids loads, especially so long as you can keep their feet on the ground.

Anyway, how do you know their friends are bad? Maybe your child has a wild streak that needs to be indulged, even if you don't share it or like it. And perhaps that kid who smokes is also tremendously loyal. The child who plays with your daughter's emotions might also stick up for her in front of the class bully. Or be able to make her laugh when she's having a bad day. You don't have to put up with your child smoking or vandalising cars of course, but the friends who do so may still be valuable as friends.

Personally, although I have favourites among my children's friends, I'm happy to put up with all of them. Even the ones I like least clearly give my kids something worth having. It's just some of the parents I have a problem with.

> # HOW DO YOU KNOW THEIR
> # FRIENDS ARE BAD?

---

[*] Although not as much French, obviously.

Remember you're their parent, not their teacher

Obviously you want your kids to do well at school, pass their exams with good grades and you may even be thinking ahead towards them getting a place at one of the better universities. So it can be really tempting to get heavily involved in their schooling – whether that's checking what homework they've been given or wanting to add your knowledge to theirs.

One dad I know regularly asks his children what topics they've covered at school that week and then spends half the weekend trying to tell them everything he knows about the subject (which he's sure is far more than the teachers know). What a brilliant way to turn your kids off learning and give them a severe case of overload.

Let's get this straight. Teachers are there to pass on information to your kids and coach them towards doing well in exams, which is how both children and teachers are measured. You, on the other hand, are not your child's teacher. You can allow them to be wrong and to learn for themselves without correcting them. You can emphasize all those important life skills we've talked about before (try Rule 12) that school isn't there for (and which you can't measure), and that actually are far more important than academic achievement. You can encourage them to try new things (foreign holidays, karate classes, sailing, olives), discover new interests, meet new people. You can encourage them to read widely and take an interest in the world, to ask questions and form their own opinions.

School can easily dominate your child's life at times, and they need you to keep it in perspective. If you spend their time at home nagging them about their homework and asking them where they came in that week's tests or insisting on telling them everything you know about Henry VIII, school will permeate every part of their lives. And if a teacher has told them off for something, they don't need you to do it again. Once is enough. You shouldn't undermine the school (Rule 69) by suggesting you think the teacher was being petty, but you can tell your child, 'You should do as the school asks even if you disagree with it, but as you've been told off once already I'm not going to do it again', and then change the subject.

Yes, I know they're supposed to do their homework, and if you don't ask where their dirty games kit is you can't wash it (and you can't be expected to know their socks are in their pencil case), but let them escape from school as much as possible. The older your child gets, the more dominant school will become, with longer hours and more homework and more exam pressure, so it becomes ever more important for you to give them a chance to get away from it when the bell goes.

This doesn't mean you can't show a healthy interest in what they are doing at school, or discuss topics with them if they seem keen. No, it just means giving them a bit of peace and space and helping broaden their horizons by thinking about or doing other stuff.

> ## SCHOOL CAN EASILY DOMINATE YOUR CHILD'S LIFE AT TIMES, AND THEY NEED YOU TO KEEP IT IN PERSPECTIVE

Don't mollycoddle them

I bet there are some kids in your child's class who are almost never there. Especially in the winter. They're always off school for coughs or colds or imaginary allergies,* being wrapped in cotton wool by their parents. And when they are at school, they're off games or swimming because they've got a bad finger or they felt a bit sick yesterday morning. I went to school with someone who stayed at home whenever his hay fever got bad. Missed masses of important lessons, and his friends got used to hanging out without him all summer so he didn't fit back in come the autumn. And what was the point? He had a huge garden at home – his hay fever must have been worse than if he'd come to school with its tarmac and paved grounds.

I'll tell you something I've noticed over the years. Parents who keep their kids off school at the drop of a hat are the same people who take time off work themselves constantly because they have a headache or a cold. And their kids grow up to be the kind of people who moan and expect to be looked after every time they develop a snuffle, and turn into adults who don't believe you should go to work if you feel even slightly under par.

I've got news for those parents (not you of course, because you wouldn't do it): if you have a bit of a cold, it will be there whether you're at work or at home. So you might as well turn up to work. And the same goes for your kids. You do them no favours by training them to expect the world to stop for them every time they're a bit under the weather. And their future bosses aren't going to thank you either, as they once again regretfully pass them over for promotion because their work is great but their attendance is just too poor.

---

* Don't get me started. I know some allergies are genuine and serious. That's why I get so incensed by all the make-believe ones that undermine the credibility of the legitimate sufferers.

What happened to the good old-fashioned values of stiff upper lip, and moral fibre, and all that? We Rules parents want rough, tough kids, not whimsy little ailing butterflies. Interestingly, I've worked with people over the years who always show up even when they're unwell, and with people who take time off at the first sign of a sniffle. And you know what? The ones who keep going get ill a lot less often than the ones who feel sorry for themselves all the time.

Of course you keep your child at home if they're genuinely ill, but not otherwise. If they're fit enough to run around, they can do it at school. They should only be at home if they're actually ill enough to spend the day in bed or under a blanket on the sofa. They're missing out on their friends and their lessons, and that's not doing them any good. And let's dismiss the argument about not spreading the germs at school. Where do you think they picked up the bug in the first place? If it's mild enough to go to school with, it won't do the rest of the class any harm anyway.

So don't mollycoddle your child. Be sympathetic, certainly – it's no fun having a cold – but don't let them grow up thinking it's an excuse for a day off.

WHAT HAPPENED TO THE GOOD OLD-FASHIONED VALUES OF STIFF UPPER LIP, AND MORAL FIBRE, AND ALL THAT?

Let up the pressure

Your child is going to want to get certain grades at school. Whether it's exams or continuous assessment, whether it's just for the sake of doing well or whether they actually need the grades in order to carry on with the subject or get onto the course they want – they will have to pass, and maybe pass particularly well.

They know this. The teachers keep telling them. Their friends keep telling them. They keep telling themselves. They really don't need you to tell them as well. Too much pressure can be counter-productive, and it can cause genuine and sometimes serious psychological problems for children.

So what's your job? You need to keep things in perspective for them. When you're 16, for example, school is likely to give you the impression that your whole life hangs on your exam results. Well, chances are it doesn't.* I failed almost all my O-levels (yes, I'm old enough to have sat O-levels), and it's done me no harm. Einstein famously failed his finals. (Notice how I classed myself together with Einstein then, just to make me feel good.)

You need to think about how stressed your child is about the whole exam thing. It's quite probable that already they're feeling the pressure a bit too much, even without your contribution. So rather than adding to the pressure, you need to add a bit of perspective instead. Look, it's hard to see past the end of school when you're a kid, and your job is to reassure your child that there are more important things in life than academic achievement, and that people who fail exams are just as likely to go on to become happy, fulfilled grown-ups. Yes, if they do well in their exams that will be wonderful, but if they don't, the world won't fall apart. If the poor child is already under too much strain, then you need to

---

* Unless you are absolutely desperate to be a doctor or vet or something, in which case I admit they are rather useful.

say something to take the pressure off, and actually give them a better chance of succeeding, rather than having a breakdown. And if that means reassuring them that it'll be OK whatever happens, then that's what you do.

But suppose you think they really aren't stressed enough, that they aren't taking it all seriously, and they don't realize the implications? In that case you can highlight the implications without telling them to work harder, or questioning whether they can really afford to be watching the TV or going out with their friends. The way to do that is to ask them questions: how do you rate your chances of passing? Have you thought about what will happen if you don't pass?

In the end, though, it has to be their choice how hard they work. You can't force them. Even if you lock them in their room that's no guarantee they'll do it. So rather than add to their burden of pressure, why not be their salvation from it? The one place they can escape? And once they realize that you're not going to make them work, they're far more likely to learn self-discipline.

> # IN THE END, IT HAS TO BE THEIR CHOICE HOW HARD THEY WORK

RULE 77

They have to live with their choices (and it's OK)

When I was 16 I decided that I wanted to go into the Forestry Commission. I was accepted and just about to start my training when I suddenly announced that actually I wanted to go to art school instead. Quite a change. My mother must have had an opinion about this, but she admirably kept it to herself and supported my choice. I still have no idea which she thought would be best for me (if either).

You can't help but have an opinion about most of your child's choices if you care about them. You worry that they're choosing a subject they'll find too difficult, or they'll regret giving up Spanish, or they're only choosing physics because they like the teacher. But you can't do anything about it. You can help them (gently, without pressure or expressing a preference) to make the best decision they can, and then you have to support them in it, even if you're worried it's not the best choice.

Ask yourself a few questions too: what will happen if they don't make the choices I think they should? Do I want them to take this option for themselves or for me? I know you're a Rules parent and you wouldn't consciously try to steer your child down a career or life path that wasn't their own choice, but it's very easy to think you know best. You may think you're basing your choice on what's best for them, but even so you may not be right.

Your job as a parent, as I keep reiterating, is much broader than the school's role. You're not only teaching them chemistry or music or English. You're teaching them skills for life. And that includes stuff like decision-making. If you don't let them do it, you're not actually helping.

Incidentally, I didn't grow up to be a forester or an artist. I grew up to be lots of different things before eventually settling down to become a writer. I have a friend who agonised at school over whether to study Latin or Russian, and who now runs an employment agency. And another who couldn't decide whether to study philosophy or sociology at uni. She works for a conservation charity. I know two people with degrees in chemistry: one is a very successful merchant banker, and the other is a very successful jester (yes, honestly). I even know a 72-year-old who dropped out of school at 15 to become a customs officer, and retrained in his 60s to get a law degree and become a lawyer.

You see, our choices can have some influence on which course our lives take, but not necessarily remotely the influence we expect. So your child might as well study the subjects they want to. And if you've given them the confidence and the skills they need when they're growing up, they'll be able to turn any kind of school options and exam results into a career that will make them happy.

> # YOU HAVE TO SUPPORT THEM, EVEN IF YOU'RE WORRIED IT'S NOT THE BEST CHOICE

TEENAGE RULES

By the time you get this far, you'll be a pretty established Rules parent and you'll know what you're doing most of the time. But teenagers have a way of throwing out new challenges and making you feel clueless about how to be a good parent.

Once your child becomes a teenager, you're well over half-way through the job of raising them, and you have only a few years left to inculcate all those values and principles you want them to go into adult life with. And suddenly, they look as if they're throwing away all the work you've put in up to now.

But actually, if you just keep your head, and follow these essential teenage Rules, you'll find you come out the other end with a terrific adult you can really be proud of.

RULE 78

Don't panic

Teenagers. I've been there. And it's a scary place. Suddenly your adorably cute little child has turned into someone you don't recognize. At best they're sullen and uncommunicative, at worst they're a monster out of hell.

So the first Rule is: don't panic. It's supposed to be like this. You're not the only parent to go through this – most of us do. A few get off lightly, but if you have more than one child, it's almost unheard of to get them all through their teens painlessly. And it's probably not even healthy.

Do you remember your child going through the terrible twos? Well, now they're back – and this time they're much bigger and much scarier. The terrible twos are about your toddler realizing that they're not an extension of you and pushing boundaries to find out what they can and can't do, now they have their own minds. And the teens are a grown-up version of this. Your child has got to go their own way in life, and they have to be able to do it alone. So this is where they break free. And they don't always agree with you about how far they can stray.

Add to that all sorts of hormonal surges and swooshes and flurries, some of which actually affect their brain function and communication skills (look up the research on the internet if you don't believe me), and it's no wonder you're in for a spot of bother.

I've known kids who get the whole teenage angst thing over with by the time they're 16 or 17, and others who don't do it at all until they're in their early 20s, but almost all of them do it at some time and to some degree. Broadly speaking, the ones who enjoy being children, maybe who like being the baby of the family if they're the youngest, hit it later than the ones who've been itching to be adults since they were 2 years old. But they all have to do it if they're ever going to break free of you.

I have a friend who thought she'd got away with it when her daughter turned 18 with no visible teenage stroppiness and angst to speak of. Then bam! Six months later she became sullen and grumpy and did the whole teenage thing just as most of her contemporaries were coming out of it. You see – it's not safe to turn your back on them for a moment.

The good news is that once they come out the other side, the familiar person you knew will be back. Changed, of course – older and wiser – but still with all those values and ideals you spent so long working on intact. You just need to keep the faith and stick it out for a few years and it will all be OK.

> ## KEEP THE FAITH AND STICK IT OUT FOR A FEW YEARS

Remember Newton's Third Law

The thing is, you love your kids desperately. So it's incredibly hard to watch them making mistakes that you think will come back to bite them later on. Over the years you've got used to letting them make small mistakes – helping themselves to too much pudding, or riding their bike too fast downhill. As time goes on, the mistakes get bigger.

So now you have to watch them drink too much at their mate's party, or wear clothes that are far too low-cut (or high-cut). Maybe you even have to stand back when they decide to leave school at 16, when you'd hoped they go to university, or jack in a brilliant Saturday job because it's too much effort getting up in the morning. It's a much bigger deal than letting your 2-year-old take too much pudding. The stakes are getting higher.

And worst of all, you may even have to watch them repeating your mistakes. Dropping science just because they hate the teacher when they could have a brilliant career ahead of them. Or saving all their money for a gap year when the time comes, and then blowing it in a moment of madness on a car that doesn't even go properly. You could have told them. You probably did tell them. Quite possibly loudly and forcibly . . . But then, did you listen to your parents when *they* told you all those years ago?

Unless your child is putting themselves in serious danger, you really do have to put up with it. Sometimes even if it's dangerous you have no choice. The more you try to tell them, the more you push them in the opposite direction. They're looking for something to kick at, to rebel against, because they're programmed to. The more force you use, the more they'll use. Remember Newton's Third Law of Motion? For every action there is an equal and opposite reaction. He could equally well have called it the First Law of Teenagers.

So what can you do when you see them going wrong? You can tell them what you think, but don't tell them what to do. And tell them in the way you'd tell a grown-up and an equal. Not, 'I'll tell you what I think! I think you're a fool!' More along the lines of, 'It's your decision, but have you thought how you'll fund your gap year if you spend your money on this?' Talk to them like an adult and maybe they'll respond like an adult. And if not this time, maybe next time. They'll certainly be quicker to ask your advice if they know it will be given as an equal.

> **DID YOU LISTEN TO YOUR PARENTS ALL THOSE YEARS AGO?**

Give them a voice

Your child has got to learn how to make decisions. And how to compromise. And how to work as part of a team. And how to negotiate. And what better way to teach them than to involve them in family decisions? They need to be consulted on decisions that affect them, just as you'd expect to be.

Of course, they don't always get the casting vote. They need to understand that if it's your house, your money, you have an ultimate right of veto. But that won't always apply. In the end you can't be railroaded by your kids into building a three-bedroomed extension just because they fancy a bedroom and a study each. But you can still consult them on how to change the existing space to get the best use from it.

As kids get older they need to practise making decisions, to be consulted, and to be treated more like adults. Why shouldn't they choose what colour to paint their bedroom, especially if they're going to do it themselves? I remember one of my teenage children filling a small hole in the bedroom wall – by the time he'd finished it was lumpy and bumpy and about six inches across. I didn't smooth it off. I kept it as a memento of his first attempt at decorating. He's long since left home but the lump is still there. He's now extremely accomplished at painting and DIY, but it reminds me that you have to let your kids start somewhere.[*]

And what about family holidays, while you still have them? You'll have to set the budget, but by the time your kids are teenagers, everyone can decide collectively where to go. You can have a right of veto if you insist, but then so can they.

It's not just about learning to make decisions, of course, important though that is. It's also about getting your kids to feel involved in

---

[*] I didn't mean that to sound sentimental and sugary. I mostly keep it there so I can wind him up about it.

the family, included in choices that affect everyone. So you can apply it to setting rules too. The England World-Cup winning rugby team all sat down to agree the rules that would make them successful, and stuck to them because they had all helped formulate them (in other words, they 'owned' them, to use the yukky business jargon).

And, of course, the more opportunities you can find to treat your teenagers as responsible adults, the better your relationship will be, and the more they will be encouraged to behave like responsible adults. And that can only be a relief for everyone.

> ## IT'S ABOUT GETTING YOUR KIDS TO FEEL INVOLVED

Don't look under the mattress

Teenagers get up to things you don't want to know about. Of course, you do know about them really, which is why you're worried. If you were entirely ignorant you'd be much happier.

Look, take it from me, your daughter has gone further than you'd like with her boyfriend. Your son has watched porn. They've both tried at least a drag of a cigarette by now. And they've almost certainly been offered drugs but they won't have any evidence of it hanging around in their room so there's no point looking. Happy? Good. Now you don't need to look under the mattress or read their secret diary.

You're not going to find anything that thousands of parents before you haven't found. In fact, you're probably not going to find anything that your own parents didn't find. And what are you going to do about it – confront your teenagers? I think not. You'll severely damage your relationship and they'll just keep the stuff under the floorboards instead.

Maybe you should think back to the things you got up to as a teenager that you didn't want your parents to know about. Maybe you even get up to things nowadays that you'd rather not tell your parents. See? Your kids are just being perfectly normal teenagers. And if you don't make a big deal out of all those perfectly normal teenagery things they're getting up to, they're much more likely to come and tell you if anything gets out of hand or is a real problem for them. And that's the really important point. If you act like all that stuff under the mattress is normal, they'll feel they can talk to you without fear of an irrational response.

There's simply no point worrying yourself. By this stage you have to rely on what you've taught them over the last dozen years or so. And follow Rule 79 – the more of a hard time you give them, the worse they'll get. So don't give them a hard time.

And, on the plus side, the very fact that you don't look under their mattress or read their diary will strengthen your relationship with them. They'll respect you for preserving their privacy (obviously they won't say this), and for having a realistic and modern enough outlook to let them get on with being teenagers undisturbed.

> **TEENAGERS GET UP TO THINGS YOU DON'T WANT TO KNOW ABOUT. OF COURSE, YOU DO KNOW ABOUT THEM REALLY, WHICH IS WHY YOU'RE WORRIED**

RULE 82

Running round after them doesn't help anybody

You started off with 18 years and counting. How many have you got left? Because once you get to zero, they'll be on their own. That means they'll have to know how to shop, cook, clean and tidy (up to a point anyway), do their own washing, pay their bills, stay in the black, and all the rest of it.

I know parents – and without wanting to be sexist here it's almost always mothers – who are still looking after their kids when they're 18. And the kids, not being daft, let them do it. In fact, I have one friend who is 35 and still takes his washing to his mother's. I don't mean he borrows his mother's washing machine, which might be understandable, I mean he hands the washing to his mother and leaves her to get on with it. It takes two to play that game.

You're counting down the last few years now to independence. And if your child hits 18 never having used a washing machine or cooked a decent meal, is that really fair on them? They may not realize what a handicap it will be, but you know perfectly well, as a Rules parent, that mollycoddling a child doesn't prepare them for the real world (see Rule 75).

You know your child's strengths and weaknesses as well as anyone. So think through what they still need to learn, and make sure they do. If they're hopeless with money, teach them to budget. Get them to do the family shopping for a week on your usual budget, or get firm about not paying to top up their mobile beyond the agreed amount.

Put them in charge of the family's washing for a week (maybe liberate them from washing-up for the week to compensate) so they learn to use the machine and find out what a drag it is to have to hang it all up and fold it all again later (it might even make them think twice before dropping barely worn clothes in the laundry basket).

You could even leave older teenagers to housesit while you go away for a few days. Yes, I know what you're thinking. And yes, you'll have to come up with a good enough incentive for them to resist the temptation to invite all their friends round for a wild party. And let them know a neighbour or friend is keeping an eye on them.

Come on, you can be inventive about finding interesting ways to teach them vital skills, which should be reasonably entertaining for them – at least until the novelty wears off, by which time they should have learnt something.

> ## YOU'RE COUNTING DOWN THE LAST FEW YEARS NOW TO INDEPENDENCE

Don't stand in front of a speeding train

You already know your children need to be allowed to make their own mistakes (Rule 79). So far, so good. Now, how many of these decisions are you going to let them make for themselves:

- Riding a motorbike?

- Playing truant?

- Using the F-word?*

- Trying drugs?

- Smoking?

- Having sex before they're 16?

Hmmm, yes, tricky. It gets harder, doesn't it? Are you seriously supposed to let them do all of that? Well, let's look at it another way: how are you going to stop them? Your options are getting pretty limited these days. You can yell at them (see Rule 84), but that doesn't bother them as much as it did when they were 5 years old. And anyway, they can yell back louder these days. You can ground them, but any teenager worth their salt will climb out of the window, or at least play good until you finally let them out again, and then just be more careful not to get caught. You can refuse to fund them, but they're old enough to earn their own money these days.

I know someone whose father actually disinherited him (they were an extremely wealthy family) just for shaving his head. Even

---

* My mother had a great system. When you were 14 you were allowed to use mild swear words, when you were 16 you were allowed to use the F-word, and when you were 18 you were allowed to say the C-word. Quite hard to keep track of with six of us, but she managed it.

that didn't encourage him to grow his hair back. That's teenagers for you – if being deprived of a potential seven-figure fortune doesn't motivate them, nothing will. (As it happens the father died suddenly before he'd calmed down enough to write his son back into the will, and the son really did lose that fortune.)

So basically, you've got no choice. Your teenager is going to behave like a teenager no matter what you do. You can either accept it or fight it, in which case they're even more likely to make the decisions you don't want them to.

Oh, and of course, there is one other thing you can do: trust them. All kids get offered things their parents don't want them doing – sex, drugs, fags. But if you trust your child to make responsible decisions for themselves, there's a good chance it will work. And if it doesn't, nothing else would have worked either. Trust me.

> ## YOUR TEENAGER IS GOING TO BEHAVE LIKE A TEENAGER NO MATTER WHAT YOU DO

RULE 84

Yelling isn't the answer

Suppose your child has done all those things in Rule 83. OK, that's too awful to contemplate. Suppose they've done just one or two of them. And things have gone wrong. They can't kick the fags, or they've got an STD, or they're about to get expelled from school. Would you rather they came to you for help, or not?

Of course you would. No question, you want to help. But are you sure they're going to tell you? How will they decide whether to tell you or not? The answer is, they'll judge by what's happened in the past when you've found out about things. Smaller things probably – the time they spilt paint all over the bedroom carpet, or that time they promised they'd arranged a lift home from the party and then you found out they'd hitched.

How did you react then? Did you shout and yell and scream at them and tell them how they'd let you down and couldn't possibly be trusted? Or did you discuss it seriously and calmly and explain why you were so concerned?

The fact is that shouting and screaming and telling them how they've let you down may well be totally justified BUT it has the opposite effect to the one you want. If you want them to come to you when they're in trouble, they have to know that you'll take things seriously but you won't yell at them. You might not like that, but that's the way it is. You must have felt pretty much the same when you were a teenager. If your parents were yellers, I bet you didn't tell them half as much as your friends with calm parents told theirs.

Chances are, you see, they already know they've done something wrong or stupid, and they may be embarrassed or ashamed of it. They really don't need you to shout at them and add to the humiliation. In fact, if your reaction is calm and doesn't belittle them, they may even be pathetically grateful to you. And that really racks up points in your favour for next time something goes wrong.

Remember, your kids are going to gauge your reaction by how you react to minor troubles today and tomorrow and next month. Basically, once your kids reach a certain age, you have to change your whole parenting style. You can't keep telling them what they must and mustn't do. You have to turn into more of a mentor, an adviser. So by the time they're 18 you can treat them pretty much as an equal. Sure, when they're in your house, your house rules apply. But so they should to your friends and even your parents. In terms of what your kids do with their life, you have no control so there's not much point pretending you have. And that's pretty well true by the time they reach their mid-teens. So give up the yelling, and start talking to them like adults. It can be really tough, but it's the only way that works.

> ## BASICALLY, ONCE YOUR KIDS REACH A CERTAIN AGE, YOU HAVE TO CHANGE YOUR WHOLE PARENTING STYLE

Let them have the last word

Oooh, this is difficult sometimes. But you have to pick your battles, and you don't want to get sucked into a yelling session – as we've just established.

Not every conversation you have with your teenager is going to end amicably. I think you know that. Which means that when you finish a tricky discussion (or your teenager finishes it for you by walking off) there's likely to be a petulant or cantankerous or snappy or sarky closing remark from one of you. Replied to by the other. And thrown back again . . . and so on. Oh, look – you haven't finished the discussion after all. Not that it's very constructive any more. In fact, it's descending into one of those yelling matches we just decided to avoid . . .

Hold up there. Enough. Stop. Well, someone has to. All teenagers are masters of the last word – always designed to sting you into a retort. Don't fall for it. Don't let them suck you back in. And don't, whatever you do, launch into some petty, pointless and unnecessary debate about not being lippy or not talking back.

Someone has got to resist having the last word here. So the only question is which one of you should it be? Should it be:

(a) the one with years of experience and a mature overview of what's going on, or

(b) the one with way less experience, masses of stroppy hormones slopping around inside them, and a reputation as a fully fledged teenager to maintain?

I'm not going to patronise you by answering that question for you, and I'd just like to point out that if *you* can't resist having the last word, I don't see how you can criticise your teenager for giving in to the temptation. It's a hard thing to do, I grant you (indeed I'm mostly writing this Rule so I can read it back to myself repeatedly until it sinks in). But it's a great example to set your child – the ability to keep your mouth buttoned. So show them how to do it, and keep the moral high ground at the same time.

The last word thing is a lot about feeling that you've 'won' or saved face. Letting the other person get the last word in can seem tantamount to admitting they've won the argument. The only way I can keep shtum is by deciding in advance that I'm going to have more self-control than them, and to demonstrate it by *not* having to have the final word. This means that I feel in control when I choose not to respond, which psychologically puts me back on top. At least in my own petty little world. It works though – and it makes a lot of arguments with teenagers a lot shorter, which has to be worth it.

> # DON'T, WHATEVER YOU DO, LAUNCH INTO SOME PETTY, POINTLESS AND UNNECESSARY DEBATE ABOUT NOT BEING LIPPY

RULE 86

Everything comes with strings

One of the most essential things your children have to learn in life is that rights and responsibilities are inextricably linked. And it's your job to teach them. Or should I say your responsibility?

For example, your children can demand the right to be treated like adults. But they need to understand that the right comes with a responsibility to behave like adults. If they duck the responsibility, they lose the right.

Once your children become teenagers this principle can really kick in. For every right they demand (and, boy, do teenagers like demanding rights), you can point out to them the responsibility that goes with it. I have friends who extend this to pocket money. Their kids have the right to a certain weekly allowance, but their parents explain that they also have a responsibility to the household. This means there are certain basic chores that have to be carried out for the house to run smoothly – clearing the kitchen after meals, keeping mess to a minimum and so on. If the kids shirk this responsibility, they lose the pocket money.

The same goes for the right to be treated with respect. It goes with the responsibility to treat others with respect. If your kids swear at you or yell at you, they lose the right to your respect. You can stop listening to them (or at least try to block out the sound) until they can be respectful.

Once your children get out into the big wide world they're going to need to know this stuff. They can't expect something for nothing. And the teenage years are the perfect opportunity to learn the relationship between rights and responsibilities. Everything your kids want comes with strings: respect, money, independence, freedom, status. Indeed responsibility itself comes with responsibilities.

And actually, kids like this stuff. They really do. It shows you care. When you tell your kids they can't stay out late unless they can be responsible about letting you know where they are and when they expect to be back, they're secretly rather pleased you care. They won't tell you that, though. But they will tell you when to expect them home, because they realize they'll lose the right to be out late again if they don't.

So do your kids a favour and don't let them off the hook. Every time they want something from you, let them know what you expect in return. It will teach them the value of rights, and prepare them for the future. And it should make your life a good deal easier too.

> THE TEENAGE YEARS ARE THE PERFECT OPPORTUNITY TO LEARN THE RELATIONSHIP BETWEEN RIGHTS AND RESPONSIBILITIES

Show some respect for the things they care about

I know a man who started to develop psychological problems as a teenager. He used to spend as much time as he could in his bedroom listening to music, which was the one thing that really gave him pleasure. As time went on things became worse. Even after he'd left home the problems continued. Many years later he said a very interesting thing. He explained that one of the biggest blows to his confidence was the way his parents used to bang on about the awful music he listened to.

You see, when you criticise your teenager's choices, you criticise them. It's an age of fragile egos and easily knocked self-esteem, and it's easy to make your teenager feel that you disapprove, or even that you don't like them. Whether it's their music or their politics or the way they dress or their decision to become vegetarian, they need to know that it's OK with you.

It's one of the many paradoxes of teenagers. On the one hand they want to rebel, to shock you, to do things that really get to you, and on the other hand they want your approval and your goodwill. I know it's confusing for you, but it's worse for them. They're trapped inside minds and bodies that are trying to make the transition from dependent child to independent adult, and they don't know what they want themselves half the time. One minute they want to grow up as fast as possible, and the next it's all getting too scary and they want to slow down. You just have to accept it and go with the flow.

Meantime, take an interest in the things that they enjoy. They may not show it, but actually they'll think that's pretty cool. No need to go over the top – in fact please don't, as there's nothing worse than a forty-something dad pretending he's into the latest dance music scene. Don't try too hard – you're just showing an interest here. You don't have to pretend to be a huge fan of their music or clothes style, but you don't have to put it down either. And actually, you might even discover all sorts of new things to enjoy. That's one of the many plus sides to having a teenager: they're close enough to adulthood to have some pretty sophisticated interests, and you can learn a lot from them if you're broad-minded enough. And of course you are.

> # I KNOW IT'S CONFUSING FOR YOU, BUT IT'S WORSE FOR THEM

Adopt a healthy attitude to sex

No, not your own sex life. I hope that's already healthy. I mean sex in general and, in particular, your teenager's sex life. They may not have one yet (are you sure?) but they will do sooner or later. And you want to make sure that when they do, it's happy and safe and fulfilling, not furtive and dirty and messy (oh alright, it's always messy).

What is the single factor most likely to give your teenager a good experience? And, indeed, the confidence to delay that first experience until they're ready? That's right: being comfortable with the subject. The more your child knows about sex and finds it easy to talk about, the more able they will be to say no, or to insist on a condom, or to respect their partner's feelings.

You can pretty much take it as read that the more you talk about sex (and drugs, alcohol, smoking and all the rest) at home, the more confident your teenager will be in making mature decisions for themselves when the time comes. Even broad-minded parents who report strong relationships with their teenagers generally say that this is the trickiest subject to discuss comfortably, probably not least because teenagers also report that they find it difficult. But the onus is on you to show that it's a perfectly acceptable, normal thing to talk about.

School will teach your child the mechanics of sex, of course, and very probably also the basics of HIV and STDs and how to put on a condom. But your kids will giggle their way through this with their friends and it won't tell them anything about the fact that sex is a normal part of adult life, and that it has a complex relationship with the emotions. You'll have to tell them that – don't count on school to do it.

This doesn't mean you have to sit your child down for a formal talk about sex. I did actually try to broach the subject formally with one of my children – probably far too late, in hindsight – and asked him at the end if there was anything he needed to know. He replied: 'No thanks, Dad. And anyway, it's all changed since your day.' I was surprised and intrigued to hear this, but he frustratingly refused to be drawn further.

There's nothing wrong with a formal chat if you can do it without cringing, but sex still needs to be a part of everyday conversation when it crops up, discussing a film or a news story or a friend's exploits. Instead of hastily changing the subject in your teenager's presence, carry on, and even ask their opinion. Just make sure you always put across a responsible viewpoint. I don't necessarily mean no sex until you're married; I mean that it's not right to mess with other people's emotions, or to take risks with their health.

> # MAKE SURE YOU ALWAYS PUT ACROSS A RESPONSIBLE VIEWPOINT

CRISIS RULES

It would be lovely if you could get your kids through their childhoods without ever having to deal with a real crisis. But, sadly, very few parents manage it. It could be divorce, severe illness, financial disaster, the death of one of the family, serious bullying at school, redundancy, house repossession. These situations are generally a major problem for you as a parent in themselves, as well as giving you cause to worry about your child.

You might have all sorts of brilliant strategies, techniques, house rules and policies that mean you sail through most everyday problems with the kids. But when this kind of crisis hits, you are often completely unprepared, and the normal systems don't seem to be enough. And you may well be in shock or panic or a state of depression yourself, and possibly even suddenly coping with the kids on your own, in which case you'll probably need a little help to get through.

So if the worst happens, here are a few overarching Rules to help you deal with the situation, and reassure you that you're on track. You will get through it, if only because there's no choice, and your children will learn from it. You can make sure that they come through it stronger and more understanding of other people's problems for having had first-hand experience themselves.

RULE 89

Don't use your kids as ammunition

This applies chiefly to parents going through a divorce, of course, but it's a trap you can also fall into if there's a strain on your relationship during other kinds of crisis. When your emotions are heightened, they all tend to be heightened. So whether you're deeply upset, desperately worried, seriously depressed or unbearably sad, it's likely that any time you feel angry you will feel almost uncontrollably angry. That might be all the time or only some of the time, but when you feel angry you feel compelled to call on every argument or tactic you possibly can.

Unfortunately, one of the strongest tactics you can use is to play on your partner's (or ex-partner's) love for their kids. Your kids. You may be able to restrict their access to them. Or only allow access at times you know will really inconvenience them. Or give them the shortest possible notice of your plans. Or even drop little remarks to your kids to undermine their feelings for the other parent. Or subtly let your kids know that your happiness depends on them.

You may have encountered some or all of these tactics being used against you by your partner. That makes it very tempting to fling the same things back at them. After all, they started it, didn't they?

Actually, does it matter who started it? I don't mean to you, I mean do the kids care who started it? All they care is that it stops. They're not fools, and they know what's going on, at least in part. They know they're stuck in the middle, between two parents they love, and the situation is bad enough already without all this. What they *don't* know is how to handle serious conflict, but they're learning fast by watching you and their other parent. Are you sure you're teaching them what you want them to learn?

It is incredibly hard to avoid playing these games when your partner or ex is playing them. But you have to resist the temptation.

It's essential that you keep the moral high ground (see Rule 94 in *Rules of Life*). Yes, I know it's as difficult as it is important, but you're a Rules Player and you can do it. You must do it. Return every belligerent and nasty ploy with calmness, decency, honesty and integrity. Make yourself proud of yourself.

A friend of mine, who fortunately happens to be a consummate Rules Player, was going through a very difficult time with her husband. One day her son suddenly announced that his father had said he could have a motocross bike for his 14th birthday, when both parents had always agreed that this was something to wait until 18. It was clearly a ploy to get at her, and get closer to the son by buying his affection. Out of sheer frustration, my friend was so tempted to tell her son exactly what she thought of his low-life father. Instead she said nothing to her son, demanding huge self-restraint, but took it up with her husband in private. Using extreme diplomacy, and making her tongue bleed by biting it so hard, she resolved the situation by compromising on the 16th birthday, but in the meantime her husband could take their son to motocross events one weekend a month.

And what's the payoff? Your kids will understand – one day, if not yet – that you did it for them. It will strengthen your relationship with them and, best of all, it will make them much, much happier than the alternative. And surely that's a better feeling than any petty satisfaction you can gain from putting one over on their other parent?

> # DOES IT MATTER WHO STARTED IT? I DON'T MEAN TO YOU, I MEAN DO THE KIDS CARE WHO STARTED IT?

Let them cope in their own way

When I got divorced many years ago from my first wife, I ended up as a single parent with almost nothing. The kids and I were in a rented house with very little furniture. One evening I was talking to one of my sons – we were both sitting on boxes and I was overcome with guilt at what the kids were having to go through. I said to him, 'I'm really sorry, mate. I'm so sorry you have to go through all this.' Do you know what his reply was? He said, 'No, Dad. It's brilliant! This is really good fun!'

Of course he didn't mean that he wanted his parents to split up. But I was worrying about the living conditions, while he felt as if he was on a permanent camping holiday. I'd just assumed he'd feel the same way as I did, but I couldn't have been more wrong.

It can work the other way round too. Sometimes kids feel things much more deeply than us. You might remember that when you were called names at school you just brushed it off. But that doesn't mean your child can necessarily do the same. Maybe you aren't bothered that you have to relocate with your new job but your teenage daughter might be devastated. And her emotional trauma is genuine and has to be taken seriously. It's not enough to tell her to toughen up, or that she'll make new friends, or there's always texting, Facebook and Twitter ('and we didn't have that in my day').

When you're dealing with your child's emotions, and especially during any kind of crisis, it is completely irrelevant how *you* feel. Their feelings are the only things that matter. Focus on your child and forget about yourself. I have a very dear friend whose partner died suddenly. The children reacted with varying degrees of obvious grief when she told them, but later that day all of them were, at times, laughing and playing. She told me that it was initially almost as hurtful to see them looking happy as it was to see them unhappy. But children cope differently with grief, and it's no good trying to equate their reaction with your own.

When it comes to the big stuff in life, don't make any assumptions about how your kids will cope. Rely on them to tell you how they feel, and then don't assume that they'll need the same support you would. They might want to be surrounded by friends where you'd prefer to be left alone. They might want to go on that holiday you can't face, or to cancel that party you wanted to go ahead with. If you have more than one child, they probably won't feel the same as each other. All of these things can lead to difficult choices and compromises, and only you can decide whether to do things their way or yours when there's a conflict. The vital thing is to take their feelings and coping mechanisms as seriously as you do your own or anyone else's.

> RELY ON THEM TO TELL YOU
> HOW THEY FEEL, AND THEN
> DON'T ASSUME THAT THEY'LL
> NEED THE SAME SUPPORT
> YOU WOULD

Being younger doesn't necessarily speed everything up

There's a strange school of thought I've often encountered that seems to be of the opinion that children get over things more quickly than grown-ups. I've no idea where it comes from but I can tell you it's a load of rubbish.

Of course, some kids get over some things more quickly than some grown-ups. But children are also more likely to revisit traumas as they grow. After all, they're developing all the time and events from their past shift in significance. A child who initially seemed to cope well with a death in the family may suffer huge grief over it a few years later. Something that was said to your child five years ago might still haunt them. Or they might secretly still hope their parents will get back together, and be devastated every time something happens that seems to drive this hope further off.

We grown-ups aren't perfect, far from it, but most of us, most of the time, manage to deal with things once, work through them and come out the other side. The sadness or pain may never entirely leave us, but we learn to live with it. It's much harder for kids. As they change, so past events repeat on them emotionally. They may recover from the initial shock faster than us (or they may not), but they have very little experience in coping with their emotions and it can take them longer than us to work out how they feel and what they're going to do about it.

So let's hear no more of this nonsense about kids getting over things faster than adults. Rules parents know better than that, so don't let anyone get away with such absurd platitudes.

Your kids are going to need your help. If you have a sudden loss of financial status, for example, that can have a huge impact on your kids. They can no longer keep up with their friends over holidays, trainers, mobile phones, the car they get picked up from school in – for some kids that can be devastating. You're struggling to manage on a much tighter budget, while they've just lost half their friends, their self-confidence, their status, their dignity and their holiday. That's going to take time to recover from, even if the family were to regain its financial stability.

Let your kids know you understand that their feelings and problems may be different from yours, and that you take them as seriously as you take your own worries. You can't give them back their budget, their happily married parents, their sibling or parent who has died, their health, or whatever it is that they've lost, but you can let them know that you take them seriously and you don't expect them to recover from it faster than they are able to.

WE GROWN-UPS AREN'T PERFECT, FAR FROM IT, BUT MOST OF US, MOST OF THE TIME, MANAGE TO DEAL WITH THINGS ONCE, WORK THROUGH THEM AND COME OUT THE OTHER SIDE

The aftershock can last forever

Of course, eventually your children should get over their crises, or at least come to terms with things. In time they'll come to accept – as we all do – that their parents are divorced, or that someone has died. If they've been through illness or injury, they'll learn to cope with the fact that they have lost a limb or can't eat everything their friends can. If they've had to relocate with you, they'll make new friends sooner or later, and settle in at their new school.

But that doesn't mean that it's all over with. Some crises pass and leave you back where you started, but most leave you somewhere a little bit different. Sometimes very different. A child may have come to terms – as much as you ever can – with the death of a parent, but they will forever be a child growing up without a father or a mother. That still sets them apart, and will always carry disadvantages over and above the initial trauma. Every school sports day or prize-giving will be different for them, every birthday, Christmas or family event will have something missing.

The same goes for divorce. Just because your child accepts that you are no longer together, and may even be relieved to be past the emotional splitting-up stage, they still have to spend the rest of their childhood with parents who live in different houses and don't communicate as well as they once did. Holidays won't be the same. School plays will involve uncomfortable arrangements to make sure the parents don't meet, or embarrassing encounters if they do. And your child will have to learn to accept their parents' new partners, maybe even step-parents.

Maybe your child has been through illness or injury. I know a 3-year-old who had to have his leg amputated after a car accident. He seems to have coped remarkably well and bravely, but he will always be a child with a leg missing. That will affect what activities he can take part in – whether he's unable to or whether he becomes driven to outperform everyone else to prove himself – and it could mark him out for bullying as he gets older, or for being pussyfooted around. Whatever the effects, positive or negative, it will be different from growing up with the usual two legs.

As a parent you will no doubt be aware, often painfully so, of the long-term changes for your child. But not everyone else will be and that can be hard to take. Sometimes you'll have to point it out (maybe when you feel you shouldn't have to), and sometimes you'll need to give your child extra support and let them know that you know. Big crises will affect your child for life, but be reassured that some of the changes may be positive, even in a bad situation. Your child may become more independent, or more empathetic, or tougher, and that can be for the best.

> SOME CRISES PASS AND LEAVE YOU BACK WHERE YOU STARTED, BUT MOST LEAVE YOU SOMEWHERE A LITTLE BIT DIFFERENT

Tell them what's going on

Children can be very naïve. Hardly surprising really. Young children especially may not understand or even know what divorce or bankruptcy or death are all about. However, they are uncannily clever at picking up on stray emotions wafting around the place. They know when something's up, even if they don't know what it is.

Whether someone is frighteningly ill, or you and your partner are rowing (even under your breath or only when the kids are out), or you're terribly worried about money or work, the kids will know. Of course they won't know the details – not unless you tell them – but they'll get the gist.

Which is why you should tell them. Otherwise they'll have no choice but to make up their own explanations, and often they'll be worse than the reality. Your teenagers might well construe arguments between their parents and a heavily charged atmosphere as indicating imminent divorce – when actually you may be arguing about money but have no thoughts of divorcing over it. They might have got wind that someone is worryingly ill and think it's you, when in fact it's their granny or granddad. Still bad, but from their point of view much better than *you* being at death's door.

Look, not telling your kids when bad stuff is going on will only make things worse. You can't hide it from them, so best not to try. Of course, you don't have to give them all the nitty-gritty if that's not appropriate, but at least give them the general picture.

You'll have to use your judgement about exactly when and what to tell them, and their age will also make a big difference. You wouldn't tell a 2-year-old as much as you'd tell a 15-year-old. As a general guide, tell them the minimum and then answer their questions. The older they are, the more questions they're likely to ask. If the situation is really emotional and painful for them, don't give them more information than they ask for – they probably aren't asking because they don't want to know. They'll ask when they're ready to hear the answer.

As for when you tell them, you need to tell them once they've noticed that something's up. Don't kid yourself they haven't noticed because you don't want to have to broach it – be brutally honest with yourself. Older kids will be dropping loads of clues anyway, from snide comments ('I'm always the last to know anything') to straight questions ('Is everything OK?'). And if the bad news is inevitable – someone in the family has a terminal illness, for example – give them time to get used to it rather than telling them at the last minute.

All the best parents I know make it a principle not to hide things from their kids, but instead keep them in the loop and stick to honest, simple accounts of what's going on. It's up to you of course, and you can choose to try and keep their lives unaffected, but chances are you'll struggle and they'll find out eventually, and maybe make it much harder because it's a sudden shock instead of something they've had time to get used to. Your kids are part of the family, and anything that affects the family unit will affect them. So I'd say they have a right to know.

> ## NOT TELLING YOUR KIDS WHEN BAD STUFF IS GOING ON WILL ONLY MAKE THINGS WORSE

RULE 94

Teach them to fail successfully

No one likes to fail, but for kids it can sometimes seem even worse than it does from where we're standing. It's a sad fact that some kids even commit suicide due to the fear of failing exams, when we grown-ups know that failing exams just isn't that dreadful. Inevitably your child will fail at something sooner or later. Maybe they're brilliant at exams but they may fail their driving test, or not get into the football team, or be told they can't join their mates' band because they can't sing in tune (I've been there).

Now, as I say, you might be able to see that it's not the end of the world. But the reason this Rule is in the 'crisis' section is because, to your child, it may well be a crisis. And if they've just flunked all their GCSEs it may well be a crisis to you too. But even if you're secretly relieved they didn't make the rugby team, you still have to see it the way they do if you're going to help them cope.

If you tell your child it's not that important, it doesn't really matter, they can try again, there are other things they can do . . . you are in effect telling them that their feelings are wrong and they shouldn't be so upset. Belittling their feelings will make them feel hurt and isolated. It won't make them think, 'Oh yes, of course, silly me. It doesn't matter after all'.

So what are you supposed to do? Tell them they're right to feel devastated and it really is the end of the world? Not quite, but almost. You have to give them permission to feel as bad as they do by telling them you can see how shattered they must be, and you're not surprised they feel the way they do. Be sympathetic and understanding. You know – a few hugs and cups of tea. And a chocolate biscuit if you have one. Maybe their favourite comfort food for dinner to let them know you're thinking of them. Once you've allowed them to be miserable for a while, then they'll be ready to start climbing up out of their swamp of despair, and when they do, you'll be there to give them a leg up and point out the compensations – but only at the speed they want to hear them.

Whether your 5-year-old missed out on first place in Reception sports day, or your 17-year-old has failed to get into the university they want, if they see it as a crisis so must you.

BELITTLING THEIR FEELINGS
WILL MAKE THEM FEEL HURT
AND ISOLATED

It's better to agree than to be right

Divorce is perhaps the most frequent major crisis for children, at least in the western world, and this Rule is really specifically for parents during divorce (or the equivalent if you're not actually married). It's very easy to see divorce as something that happens between two people who were together and aren't any more. Of course, you know your kids are a factor, but they seem to be in the next sphere of ripples out from the central event.

It's more realistic to see divorce as something that happens to the whole family, and the kids are as central to it as anyone else. They may not be the ones making the decisions, but they are just as involved. What's more, however bad divorce is, most parents choose it because it's at least better than the alternative of staying together. For the kids, however, there may be no plus side at all to their parents' split. It may well seem like the worst option of all.

So making the divorce as bearable as possible for the kids, who are helplessly stuck in the crossfire of your decisions, is paramount. And the most important thing you can do for them is to agree as much as possible with your partner. Whether you're discussing who gets what, what happens to the house, child custody or anything else, do your utmost to reach an agreement. And that means even when you know it's not fair.

You might be perfectly justified in taking your ex to the cleaners, fighting them for every penny they've got, demanding to keep the house, asking for a higher share of their income . . . but actually, none of that matters as much as agreeing with them, finding an amicable working arrangement with them, and letting the kids get back to rebuilding their lives.

This one can be really tough, especially when you feel – quite rightly for all I know – that you've been appallingly mistreated and are being hammered by your ex. I know justice and revenge can taste very sweet, but surely they can't be worth having at the expense of your kids? Of course they can't. This is one of those things that really sorts the Rules from the non-Rules parents. Before you do or say anything rash, stop and think about whether this is really going to help your kids. And if you can't honestly answer yes, don't do it.

> JUSTICE AND REVENGE
> CAN TASTE VERY SWEET,
> BUT SURELY THEY CAN'T
> BE WORTH HAVING AT THE
> EXPENSE OF YOUR KIDS?

All of your actions speak louder than any of your words

Here's a Rule that doesn't only apply in a crisis, but that's when it becomes hugely important. You know they say kids never listen? Well, it's not true, but it is true that they take less note of your words than they do of the way you behave. Kids can spot hypocrisy at 100 paces, and they won't put up with it. They'll judge you by your actions.

I'm not just talking about negative words and actions. I'll give you an example. Suppose you have the sense to understand that it's good to let your emotions out and have a good cry. You can tell your children that as often as you like, but if they see you going through the same trauma and never crying, they'll find it a lot harder to follow your words than they will if your actions back them up. If it's really OK to cry (which it is, of course) then show them. Let them see you tearful and unembarrassed by it.

I have friends who fell on hard times a few years ago when the husband lost his job. They kept telling their two teenage kids there was no shame in having less money than other people, and not to be uncomfortable about being unable to afford some of the things their friends had. On one occasion the family went to lunch with some very wealthy friends, and the parents parked the car round the corner so their hosts wouldn't see what a beat-up old wreck they drove. I can promise you the teenagers spotted the hypocrisy of this instantly. I know, because it was the kids that told me about it.

It's an example of that classic parental line: 'Do as I say, not as I do.' There's no excuse for ever saying this to your child. If you can do it yourself then do it. If you can't, why expect the kids to?

Your kids will watch how you cope in difficult situations, and they will take that as their cue.. Whether you are jealous, angry, petty, bickering, uncontrolled, ashamed or just plain give up, they will grow up to believe that's an acceptable way to behave, regardless of what you might tell them to the contrary. On the other hand, if you behave with dignity, integrity, humanity, consideration and courage, that will influence them more than anything you can say.

> ## YOUR KIDS WILL WATCH HOW YOU COPE IN DIFFICULT SITUATIONS, AND THEY WILL TAKE THAT AS THEIR CUE

Make sure they know they're priority no. 1

You know that your kids come first, of course they do. But do they know that? Most of the time it's not hard to give them your love and attention, but it can be very tough when your mind and your emotions are elsewhere. When you're coping with intense worry, stress or grief it's not easy to remember to put the kids first.

In those darkest moments, your usual levels of attention and patience are challenged. It's suddenly hard to find time for a bed-time story, or a cuddle, let alone a shopping trip or a spot of football practice. Just when things are at their worst, suddenly your kids are getting less of you than usual. Maybe they're getting more of your snappiness or impatience as you feel more stressed and strung out than normal, but they're getting less of your time and attention.

I know there may not be much you can do about this. There are things in life that do take up all your time and leave you short-tempered and no fun to be around. If the house is being repossessed or your mother is terminally ill or your boss is about to fire you or one of the kids is in hospital, of course you can't be your normal cheery self. No one is expecting you to.

Some crises are pretty short-lived, while others can go on for weeks or months, even years. Often you have enough to do to look after yourself. But putting the kids first can be the best thing for you too – it gives you a focus outside yourself, stops you wallowing, and is your reason to keep battling on.

And in fact, the best way to make sure the kids know they come first is to make sure they actually do. If you're trapped in self-pity and always thinking of yourself it will show. However much cause you have to be miserable, the kids will instinctively know if you're putting yourself before them. If that's not what you want, and you want them to know they come first, make sure they do, and on some level they'll understand it. They may moan from time to time that you don't do this or that like you used to, but they'll know deep down that they're still first.

It has to be true of course. No use wallowing and occasionally saying to yourself: 'Of course the kids come first.' That won't help. But if they are your first priority in every decision, and if you make sure they're getting what they need most of the time even when it's tough for you, they'll gain confidence from knowing instinctively just how much you love them.

> # IF YOU'RE TRAPPED IN SELF-PITY AND ALWAYS THINKING OF YOURSELF IT WILL SHOW

You can't fix everything

Oh, this is a toughie. What we parents want most of all is to make everything alright for our kids. If they hurt themselves, we kiss them better. If they're in trouble, we help them sort it out. If they're sad, we hug them. If someone is mean to them, we intervene.

But sometimes our kids have to face really big things that we can't sort out for them. And the feeling of being impotent to help them is a terrible one. There are few things in life worse than watching your child suffer and being unable to take away their pain. But it can happen. When someone dies, you can't bring them back however much your child misses and loves them. Sometimes your child is ill in a way you can't fix. Or their other parent leaves and just isn't there for them when they should be.

It's an important lesson for a kid to learn: stuff happens and sometimes there's nothing anybody can do. It's a tough lesson to learn the hard way when they're so young. And watching them learn it can be heartbreaking. But learn it they must, sooner or later, and you have no control over when life decides to teach it to them. All you can do is comfort them through it, but you can't stop it hurting.

So this Rule is about accepting that there's nothing you can do. It's not always your fault, and no one else could do any better than you. It's just a bummer, end of story. Don't beat yourself up, because you don't deserve it. Things are hard enough for you already. You're probably going through the same pain yourself, as well as watching your child suffer, and you really don't need to dump anything more on yourself. Just give yourself a hug and a bit of sympathy.*

---

* And maybe chocolate.

And remember, your child isn't expecting you to work miracles. They're not daft and they know there's nothing you can do. All you can do for them right now is give them your love and lots of big hugs, so just do that. It will probably help both of you to feel a little bit better.

> # IT'S JUST A BUMMER,
> # END OF STORY

GROWN-UP
RULES

You don't get to retire from being a parent. It's a job for life with no pension. Even when you're 100 your children will still be your children. And if you've done your job properly (which you will, of course), they'll still want your approval and your support.

They won't want to be treated like kids, though. Even if, to you, they still are. So you have to find a way to have an adult relationship with them which still leaves room for you to be their parent. It's a tricky balance but I know enough parents who have done it brilliantly to know it can be done.

So here are the best Rules I've picked up over the years for making sure that you're just as good a parent when your kids are 40 as you were when they were 4 or 14.

Back off

You had 18 years to get your kids to where you wanted them to be. I don't mean you got them into a job as a top lawyer, doctor, footballer or whatever. I mean you had 18 years to equip them with everything they would need to be happy in life.

Well, time's up. You've had your 18 years. Now *back off*. If they haven't learnt it by now it's too late. From here on it's up to them and you can't interfere any more. If you see them doing something you don't like, that's tough. You should have thought of that before. You missed your chance, mate.

There's only one thing left you can still teach them, and that's to stand on their own two feet without you there to lean on. And the only way you can teach them that is by backing off. The whole of the last 18 years will have been wasted if you don't give them the chance to practise everything you taught them. What was the point of teaching them to be independent, think for themselves, make decisions and all the rest of it, unless you let them get on with it?

And you know what? If you're half the Rules parent I think you are, they'll do a damn good job with you out of their hair. If you keep interfering, you're effectively saying, 'I didn't do my job properly, and you still need help'.

Besides, we all know what happens when parents interfere. It's patronising at best, and destructive at worst. It makes it impossible to have a good adult relationship with your children. Every time you interfere you're telling them they're not capable of living their lives by themselves. That won't do their confidence any good, and I doubt it's true anyway. They may not be very good at living the life *you want them to,* but if you're a decent Rules parent that won't apply.

Of course, we don't stop learning when we're 18. I expect your kids have got a lot to learn. (Maybe you have too.) I hope so, or they'll have pretty boring lives. But they have to go and learn it from somewhere else now. I don't know where – that's up to them now (that's the point). They can choose what they learn, and how, and where from, and who with.

From now on you're taking a very background role in their training. In fact, so far in the background they won't even notice it. Because your only job now is to back off. There, I'm sure you've got the point. So I'll just back off.

> # IF THEY HAVEN'T LEARNT IT
> # BY NOW IT'S TOO LATE

Wait until they ask for advice

Having read the last Rule,[*] you might be wondering what you're supposed to do if your child wants your advice. That's no problem, you can give it to them.

That was a bit easy. Hardly worth a whole Rule, was it? Which is why, as you'll have noticed, I haven't left the rest of this page blank. There are two things you need to know about giving advice to your adult kids (and anyone else, come to think of it):

- Never, ever give them advice unless they ask.

- Give them only what they ask for.

If they ask for advice, they're asking for advice. They're not asking for instructions, directions, orders, comments on their lifestyle, opinions, judgements or anything else. They're just asking for advice, plain and simple. And even then you should tread carefully.

Let's try a little exercise. Suppose your adult child asks for your advice about whether or not to take a job they've been offered. Here are some of the many things you could choose to say:

- 'It doesn't matter. You'll only jack it in after three months like you do everything else.'

- 'You'll be a fool if you don't take it.'

- 'I've never understood what you see in carpet cleaning anyway.'

---

[*] If you're reading this in order. If not, just do me a favour and go back and read Rule 99 before this one.

- 'Well, at least they won't mind you turning up with all those ghastly nose rings and tongue studs.'

I'm not going to insult your intelligence by telling you that none of those responses was OK.* The fact is that all you need do is give them advice. Actually the best way to do that without overstepping the mark is to ask them questions: 'Why does the job appeal?' 'What sort of promotion prospects are there?' 'How do you feel about a longer commute?' That sort of thing. In other words, you're helping them to find their own answers and reach their own decisions.

Advice is just that, no more. Your kids don't have to take it. So when they finally make up their minds to do the opposite of what you suggested, that's their prerogative. It doesn't mean that your advice didn't help them to make their final decision, so don't be put out or upset. Just be glad you could help.

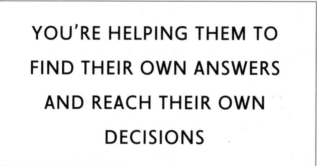

> YOU'RE HELPING THEM TO FIND THEIR OWN ANSWERS AND REACH THEIR OWN DECISIONS

---

* Whoops.

Treat them as adults

If you want an adult relationship with your adult kids, you'll need to treat them like adults. Yes, I know that sounds obvious, but actually it can be quite difficult. You've had so many years of giving them instructions, unsolicited advice, opinions, discipline and so on, that it's become your natural mode of interaction. It can be pretty hard to remember to bite your tongue until you get the hang of it.

Of course, the younger you started easing off when they were teenagers, the easier it will be now. But even so it's quite a transition to accomplish. No one's expecting you to get it right all at once. The important thing is to know where you want to get to, and not to ease up until you're there. Train yourself out of telling them what to do, or letting them know you disapprove of their taste in clothes, girlfriends or anything else.

Half of treating them as adults is about all the things you have to stop doing, from telling them how to behave to reminding them how cute they were when they were 6 (they really don't want to hear that cringe-making story yet again).

The other half of it is about the things you start doing. Talk to them about the things you talk to friends about. You have to ignore the generation gap to relate to your kids as adults, and that means valuing their opinion as much as anyone else's on climate change or the Premier League or the next election or whether to plant out your leeks yet.

And ask your kids' advice. There must be loads of things they know more about than you do. Fixing cars, fashion, photography, quilting, model railways, birdwatching, ceramics – I don't know what you're into. And technology, of course, but I'm assuming you've been asking their advice on that for years.

After a while this should become second nature, but to begin with you need to do it consciously, otherwise it just won't happen. And you have no idea how proud your kids will feel when you want their opinion and treat them like an adult – unless your parents did the same for you, in which case you'll know how important it is.

> ## TO BEGIN WITH YOU NEED TO DO IT CONSCIOUSLY, OTHERWISE IT JUST WON'T HAPPEN

Don't try to be their best friend

Now this is a mistake that many otherwise excellent parents make. It's just so tempting. After all, you love your children more than anyone (except maybe your partner, who is already your best mate) so of course you want them to be your best friend.

Ah, but your child doesn't want you as their best friend. They may not realize it, but they really don't. I have one friend who tells me proudly that she is her daughters' best friend. And she is too. She's not just saying it. She treats them as she does her best friends, and they treat her the same. She thinks it's wonderful, but I feel sorry for her daughters.

You see, they've already got best friends. Lots of them – they don't need any more. And they've got each other too. What they really need is a mother. But there's only one candidate for the post, and she's busy being their best friend.

So what's the difference? Well, you share everything with your best friend as an equal. All your worries, fears, private thoughts. And they do the same with you. Whereas a parent is someone you look up to – not superior to you but more mature, and dependable. Someone who can protect and look after you, even though you may hope never to have to ask them to. On an everyday level, you can enjoy the same things and love spending time together, but you wouldn't tell them everything, and you don't want to hear everything from them.

What if you're terribly anxious about what your kids are up to? Are you going to tell them all about it? You'd tell your best friend. Suppose you're a single parent, or you get divorced, and then meet someone new. Or maybe you have an affair. Are you going to tell your kids all the details as you would your best friend? What if your child gets mixed up in something dodgy – drugs, say, or an affair with someone married – are you going to give them the same advice you would your best friend? Are you going to confide in your children as they get older how lonely you are, or how worried about money?

The only way you can be your children's best friend in these kinds of circumstances is either by lying to them or by emotionally blackmailing them. If you tell them you're lonely, any loving child will feel they should spend more time with you, and thus feel guilty if they struggle to do so. That's not a load you want to dump on your child, even if they'd accept it willingly. And if you either lie or emotionally blackmail them, how can they come to you when they need a reassuring shoulder to cry on, or a few wise words, or someone they can depend on? You've lost all credibility as a parent when they need one.

I'm not saying that you can't have a very close relationship with your grown-up kids. Indeed I hope you will be enormously close, share similar interests and sense of humour, and spend lots of time together. I hope you will love each other even more than you both love your friends. But it won't be the same relationship.

Your kids have to separate from you as they grow up. It's their job. It's not fair on them to try to keep them tied to you, even if you do it through friendship. And you know what else? A really good adult parent/child relationship is a truly wonderful thing, and it's worth a dozen best friends any day. So why swap?

> ## YOUR KIDS HAVE TO SEPARATE FROM YOU AS THEY GROW UP. IT'S THEIR JOB

Encourage them regardless

When my daughter left school, she went to university. The uni she chose was in Manchester and I remember going to visit it with her and hoping she wouldn't choose it, but she did. She grew up in the country and I just couldn't see her in a big city so far from home. I didn't tell her that. I just did my best to encourage her to do what she thought was best. And I'm very glad I did, because I was completely wrong. She had a great time.

It would be daft to suppose that you'd think every choice any of your kids ever make is wise, from the jobs they take to who they settle down with, to the way they raise their own kids. But they're grown-ups now and they're just as likely to be right as you are. More likely, probably, because they know themselves better than you do. And the example I've just described shows you one very good reason why you should keep your opinions to yourself and encourage them anyway: you'll just look very silly when you're wrong otherwise.

Sometimes, of course, you'll be right. But if they're making a poor choice, that's all the more reason why they need your encouragement and support. After all, if you're following Rules 99 and 100 you won't tell them you disagree with their choice. So you might as well support them. The point is that it's their life and their choice, as we've already established, and your only options are to support them or to undermine them.

There's another good reason to support them as well: it means you're saved from the awful temptation of saying, 'I told you so' when it all goes wrong – which, as I hope you know, is about the worst thing you can say to your child and is unforgivable under all and any circumstances.

Some kids will be terribly upset if they think you aren't backing their choices. Others will rebel and do the opposite of what you want if they feel any pressure from you. Even without following one of these extremes, your child still needs to know you're on their side, even after they've left home. That's why it's not enough to be neutral; you need actively to encourage them.

And if you really think they're wrong? That's fine. It's OK to be wrong sometimes. And you're not encouraging your child to do the wrong thing. You're encouraging them to do what they believe is best, right or wrong.

> **YOU'RE SAVED FROM THE AWFUL TEMPTATION OF SAYING, 'I TOLD YOU SO' WHEN IT ALL GOES WRONG**

You can't choose who your children love

If you're lucky, your child will choose a wonderful, charming partner who you get on fabulously with and are delighted to welcome into the family. But don't count on it. If they do find someone fantastic, sod's law they'll probably split up.

If you have more than one child, the chances increase that at least one of them will choose to throw in their lot with someone you're not overwhelmingly happy about. Maybe you'll just find them a bit tricky, or mildly irritating. Perhaps you'll really struggle to get along with them.

It's tough when this happens, it really is. But if you trust your child, then you have to trust them to choose the best partner for themselves. They're not picking someone for you, and nor should they. Their best chance of happiness is to make a decision unencumbered by any feeling that they need to please you. So you need to keep your opinion to yourself and support your child, whether you find it hard to like the new member of your family, or whether you disapprove or worry about the consequences of their being older or divorced or gay or foreign or having children already.

There's one thing I can promise you. If you make it clear, explicitly or implicitly, that you're not happy about your child's choice of partner, you'll make things much worse. For yourself, as well as for everyone around you. You may find your child becoming more distant, as spending time with you becomes more uncomfortable. And you won't change a thing.

If your child has any sense, they'll make sure their relationship stands or falls on its own merits, not on your opinions. I've even known people fight to hold a relationship together in order (at least in part) to prove their parents wrong. Your disapproval won't break them apart – it will just make your child unhappy. Is that what you want? If it did break them apart, your child would blame you. Is that what you want? Of course it isn't, which is why you have no choice but to smile and keep your lip buttoned.

There is good news, however. There is a way to ease any problems you have, even if you can't eradicate them. A way to ensure that your relationship with your child and their partner is as comfortable as it can be. A way to retain your closeness with your child. You may be able to guess what it is . . .

Yes indeed – be as warm and welcoming as you can, and make the new partner feel part of the family. Focus on the things you like about them (come on, there's always something) and try not to dwell on your dislike or concerns. Look for the ways in which they make your child happy. OK, so they may irritate you at times, but then so do your kids, your partner, your parents. And I bet you irritate them sometimes too. It's no reason to dislike each other. If you act positive and think positive, you can't help but feel more positive.

> IF YOU TRUST YOUR CHILD,
> THEN YOU HAVE TO TRUST
> THEM TO CHOOSE THE BEST
> PARTNER FOR THEMSELVES

Leave the strings off

One of my friends has a wealthy family who helped her to buy her house by giving her a very low-interest mortgage. Recently she decided she wanted to sell her house to go and live abroad, and buy somewhere in Switzerland. Her family told her they'd call in the loan when she sold, because they didn't approve of her decision. However, if she moved to somewhere they approved of, they'd allow her to take the mortgage with her.

Please don't do this to your kids. It's patronising, controlling, and if I think about it too hard it makes me very angry. Either you trust your kids with money or you don't. If you don't, back off and let them get on with their lives alone. If you do, let them have the money and do what they like with it. But under no circumstances should you attempt to control your children's lives by giving them gifts with strings attached, whether it's money or anything else.

I've known, sadly, parents who use all sorts of levers to control their kids' lives, and money is the most common one (the other biggie comes under Rule 106 – bet you can't wait).* They pay their grandchildren's school fees, but only if they go to the school they choose. Or they help with a house or a car, but only if they approve the choice.

Others go for the halfway option. They give the kids the money, but then let them know, 'I wouldn't have given it to you if I'd known you were just going to fritter it on expensive holidays', or whatever their personal bugbear is. You just can't do this to your kids. You're not letting go of them, and you're telling them they can't run their own lives. Well, if they really can't, it's your own fault. What were you teaching them for the first 18 years of it?

Sorry – got a bit carried away there, and you're a Rules parent anyway so you wouldn't dream of doing such a thing. But let me

---

* No peeking now.

just give you two examples of friends of mine who have had a bit of money to set up trust funds for their grandchildren, demonstrating the opposing ways of doing these things. The 'with strings' version goes like this. The grandparents set up the fund with themselves as trustees. Once the children reached 18 the grandparents controlled whether they could afford a car, a gap year, a debt-free university career, a house. The parents were cut out of the deal entirely, and in some cases have disagreed with the grandparents' choices, but are powerless.

The other friends set up a trust fund for the grandchildren but not until they'd asked their children what kind of fund they wanted it to be. They then followed their wishes, and made their children trustees – not themselves – so that having set up the fund, they have no legal rights or control over it at all. And they don't ask or stipulate how and when the children release the funds to the grandchildren. That's strings-free – and it's what I call first-class Rules parenting.

> # IT'S PATRONISING, CONTROLLING, AND IF I THINK ABOUT IT TOO HARD IT MAKES ME VERY ANGRY

Don't guilt-trip them

This is the other big lever some parents use to control their grown-up children: guilt. Some of them lay it on really thick too, but our children are sensitive creatures and even the most subtle guilt-tripping makes its point.

The most common subject of these guilt trips is the amount of attention the 'child' pays to their parent. Comments like, 'Your sister phones every week' or 'I know you're ever so busy at weekends. I wish I could say the same', are all intended to make the kids feel bad about not spending more time with their parents. Even, 'Oh, it'll be so lonely here once you leave home'.

Look, let's get something straight. Your kids owe you nothing. *Nothing*. I don't care how much blood, sweat and tears went into those first 18 years of their lives. They didn't ask to be born, and having chosen to have kids, you became responsible for all that effort. You owe them loads, but they owe you zilch. So it's never OK to give your kids the impression that they owe you anything – time, attention, money or anything else.

Of course, if you're a good Rules parent your children will want to do loads for you. And the fact that they don't actually owe it to you should make it all the more precious when they choose to give it to you. Good kids will look after you in your old age because you've earned it and they love you. Some kids look after their parents out of guilt, but they don't enjoy it and they resent their parents for it, and that's not what you want. You want time and attention that your kids give you freely because you deserve it. And you'll never get that if you guilt-trip them.

You must have friends who say things like, 'I've got to go and see my father this weekend. I haven't seen him for a month', or, 'I'm busy this evening – my mum calls every Wednesday and it always takes me at least two hours to get her off the phone'. Maybe you've even said such things yourself. But you don't want your kids talking about you like that. You want them to say, 'I can't make it – I really want to see my parents this weekend' or 'I haven't spoken to Mum properly for a couple of weeks and I do miss a good chat with her'. So lay off the guilt because however much they'll do for you through guilt, they'll do twice as much without the guilt, and you'll know they're enjoying it.

In fact, the best gift of all you can give your children is independence. Not theirs; yours. If you are emotionally, socially and financially independent, you free them of all guilt. That way, anything they do for you they'll be doing out of love.

> # YOUR KIDS OWE YOU
> # NOTHING. *NOTHING*

Remember they still need you

As your kids get older and leave childhood further behind, they'll need you less and less (because you've done such a good job of raising them). But every so often, they'll need you for something. It might be money of course, especially for the first few years. It might be advice. Maybe they want you to help look after their kids, or to mind the dog when they're on holiday or help in the garden. Maybe they want the input of someone more experienced at selling a house or writing a CV or buying a car.

And then there are all the less tangible things. They still want your approval. They want you to look at their new house, or visit the new baby, or see the camper van they've converted. And although they may want lots of their friends to do these things too, that's not the same. When they were little they always showed you their paintings or their sandcastles or their new clothes. This is just the same, only bigger. They need you to let them know they're doing OK (although, of course, you're never allowed to admit that's what they're doing – and nor will they).

And, of course, from time to time they'll need you for the really big stuff. Emergency cover when they go into labour early, support through a divorce, help when the kids get seriously ill, somewhere to stay when the house gets flooded out. Those occasions when they need someone who will drop everything for them and ask questions later. If you're a Rules parent, they'll know that when the worst happens, you'll be there for them without complaint or fuss (or guilt trips).

As Robert Frost said: 'Home is the place where, when you have to go there, they have to take you in.' And that's what you need to be for your kids (with a bit more enthusiasm). Good parents are proud to be their kids' first line of support, and are happy to be able to help in a crisis, not complaining that their own lives are being interrupted.

As your kids get older they'll call on you less and less. Maybe they won't ask for anything significant from you for years or even decades. But don't be fooled into thinking that they don't need you anymore because they do. They will always need you. Just never let them know that you know it.

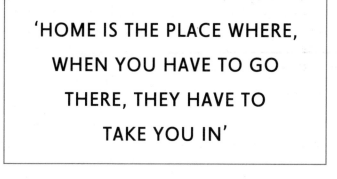

'HOME IS THE PLACE WHERE,
WHEN YOU HAVE TO GO
THERE, THEY HAVE TO
TAKE YOU IN'

It's not your fault

Some people breeze through life and some people struggle. Sometimes there's an obvious reason why they struggle, and sometimes there's no apparent reason at all. But often it's to do with the way they're made.

I've known people, as doubtless you have, from terrible backgrounds. Abuse, neglect, tragedy, you name it. A lot of them have, inevitably, been damaged by it, but many have come through stronger for it. I know a man who has no hands – he had them amputated due to illness in his late teens – and he's the cheeriest, most well-balanced fellow you could hope to meet. I know people who have had terrible childhoods grow up to be rational and happy adults. I know dysfunctional families where some kids have grown up troubled and others have come through virtually unscathed. And, conversely, I know people from wonderful families who drink, or do serious drugs, or suffer from mental illness.

Now, I have to say that I know more troubled adults from dysfunctional families than from stable backgrounds, but I still know a large number from good homes with excellent parents. Because parents are only one possible cause of adult problems. There are all sorts of other reasons why your child might have problems, both internal and external, that you have no control over.

If you know you've done your job properly as a Rules parent (remembering that you're not supposed to be perfect anyway), it's not your fault if things go wrong later. Don't beat yourself up if your child is depressive, or can't sustain a long-term relationship, or becomes alcoholic, or still hasn't got a job when they're 35. It's not your fault. You may have been responsible if they spent all night out in the rain when they were a baby, but if they sleep on the streets when they're 30 it's not down to you anymore.

The time may even come when you feel that you have no choice but to shut the door on your child. The trendy phrase is 'tough love' and certainly there are times when it's the only option left. The crucial thing is that your child knows that you're only waiting for the chance to open the door again, just as soon as you're confident that you can. If your child is really going through it, you may be the only person left in the world who is still willing to open the door. All their friends may have deserted them by now. But you are still there, still waiting, still letting them know that someone will always love them and always be on their side.

Guilt is a selfish, self-indulgent emotion, and the best way to help yourself and your child is not to wallow in how it might have been all your fault, but to accept that it isn't and focus on how you can support them now. Forget about the past and concentrate on the present. Yes, even at two in the morning when you can't sleep for worrying about them, still don't let yourself go down that road. I know it's hard but it gets you nowhere. And actually, you probably don't feel guilty because it is all your fault, but because of the fear that it *might* be. Well, if you're a half-decent parent, it isn't your fault. As the parenting author and expert Steve Biddulph says: 'Your job is simply to look after them until they can get help.'

> # GUILT IS A SELFISH, SELF-INDULGENT EMOTION

Once a parent, always a parent

Well, we've come to the end. A hundred and nine Rules. And the last Rule is that actually you never come to the end. As a Rules parent you'll have forged the most incredible relationship with a wonderful person. A relationship that is unlike any other, and that will bring both of you delight and comfort for the rest of your lives. This is the pay-off, after all those years of hard work, stinky nappies, squabbles, mess, teenage rows, sleepless nights and all the rest of it. And I promise you, it will be more than worth the effort.

You'll suddenly find you have grown-up kids who want to spend time with you, who enjoy your company, and who want to hear your opinion. They still secretly want your approval, as we've seen, although they don't want unsolicited advice. But that's fine, because you'll be full of admiration for the way they run their lives in any case. All the best parents of grown-up kids who I know spend time talking about the qualities they admire in their kids, and how they wish they could have been so confident or organized or self-possessed or clear-thinking at that age. And it's always said without the slightest hint of envy or jealousy. Rules parents say these things with nothing but pride in their voice.

Well, when you get to this stage and catch yourself thinking what amazing, incredible, wonderful people your kids are, don't forget to give yourself a pat on the back too. They wouldn't have got there without you.

One of the delights of being a Rules parent is that your child will always love you, and you'll always know it without question. And when the time finally comes when you need to depend on someone else, well, there are your kids just waiting to return the love you've given them over the years. Not because they have to, not because they owe it to you, not because you ask them, not because they feel they ought to, but simply because they want to.

> **YOUR CHILD WILL ALWAYS LOVE YOU, AND YOU'LL ALWAYS KNOW IT**

RULES ABOUT
YOUR PARENTS

Sometimes having children transforms your relationship with your own parents. With a bit of luck, everyone somehow acquires a better understanding of each other, and becomes more tolerant; after all, you're all parents now. On the flip side, it can bring a new set of challenges and expectations to tackle. Either way, you have to start doing some things differently – just at a time when you have small children distracting your attention from your parents. So having covered the Rules of being a parent, here are ten new Rules to help you manage the changes and bring the whole family closer together.

After all, there are now at least three generations of your family rubbing along together, and that can throw up unexpected challenges and surprises, and sometimes creates a triangle that you're not sure how to manage. However, you are the linchpin of this particular triangle (geometry pedants please don't write in), so it's your job to make sure everything runs as smoothly as possible.

I know some parents are trickier than others, and if you're unlucky this is never going to be easy. Nevertheless, if you, at least, are playing by the Rules, things will be a lot happier than they might. And those things include your children. Yep, the way you cope with your parents affects your children's stability and happiness, which is a big part of why it's worth making the effort with even the most difficult parents.

I've touched on various aspects of your relationship with your parents in other books, especially *The Rules of Love*, and I don't want to repeat myself. So the Rules that follow here are largely about how you relate to your parents once you are a parent yourself.

Don't put them on a pedestal

I have a friend who thinks of her own mum as pretty much the perfect parent. Her mum was enormously patient, kind and gentle; she never really got cross, she always had time to listen, she guided from the background but was never controlling, and so on. My friend loved and respected her mum and vice versa. Sounds absolutely great, doesn't it? Well it was, until my friend became a parent herself. And then? Uh oh.

You see, my friend discovered that she just couldn't replicate that relationship. And that was a massive shock. Her children are lovely but they are very different from how she was as a child. So she inevitably treats them very differently from the way her mother treated her. She knows she's not being the parent her own mother was so she wonders where exactly things have gone wrong, because this is not what she signed up for.

So what on earth *has* gone wrong? Well, nothing actually. It's all very predictable (even if she didn't see it coming). First of all times change, and you are not raising a child 20 or 30 years ago, you're doing it now. So the pressures and opportunities are different, as are the norms. Your child moves in a circle of friends and schoolmates who are not behaving as your friends and schoolmates behaved. Rules that seemed normal when you were growing up are now overly strict and stringent, and there are concerns now – for example access to the internet – that barely existed, if at all, when you were young.

Next, remember Rule 64? No? OK, it was the one about different children needing different rules. Each child is unique, and you have to take the lead from them in working out how to raise them (no, that doesn't mean they're in charge). It won't help to be hamstrung by trying to do everything your parents did with you. And the relationships are different between different children. Not to mention what happens if you have different numbers of children (my friend is one of two, and she in turn has three children and, as parents of three know, boy does that change the dynamics).

So there's the individual needs of your own child, the particular dynamics of single/dual/multiple siblings, and the fact that their generation also has its own needs. And on top of that, so do you. We all adapt our style of parenting to what works for us, and you are not your parents. Some parents love playing silly games with toddlers all day and others hate it. Some of us have a short fuse while others are endlessly tolerant. Unless you are a clone of your parent – and your partner is a clone of your other parent – what worked for them won't always work for you. So even if you have a child at the age of 18 just as your mum produces a sibling for you, and they grow up together, you still won't do it the same way.

You might be reading this Rule in utter bewilderment. Some people become parents themselves thinking their only aim is to do it all differently from the way they were brought up. However, for many people the opposite is true, and if this is you – and you think your parents did a great job – then you need to be wary of trying too hard to emulate them, or listening to every word of their advice as if it was gospel.

If your parents are truly excellent parents, they will know this and will let you alone to bring up your child in your own way. By all means ask their advice from time to time, but don't feel obliged to take it, and don't keep trying to live up to an ideal that isn't really you. You have it in you to be just as good a parent but in your own way, not someone else's.

> ## YOU HAVE IT IN YOU TO BE JUST AS GOOD A PARENT BUT IN YOUR OWN WAY

RULE 2

Let them be grandparents

I can remember the first time I watched my mother indulgently let my oldest child do something she would never have countenanced when I was a child. I was horrified. I wouldn't have let my child do it, and yet here she was, with her flagrant rule-breaking, looking as if butter wouldn't melt in her mouth.

It took me a while to get used to it, if I'm honest. In fact, I only really got to grips with it when I understood it from her point of view. She'd had years of playing bad cop as a parent. Now she wanted to be good cop for a change (or even occasionally fellow rule-breaker). She loves her grandchildren and she relishes the excuse to leave the law enforcement to someone else and to be a friend to them. She'll step in if they're becoming truly out of hand, or a danger to themselves, but otherwise she's more of a co-conspirator.

Not all grandparents adopt this particular approach, though many do. But after years as a parent it's wonderful not to have all the responsibility at last, and many grandparents behave very differently from how they did as parents. Some just stop doing things they always hated but felt obliged to do – playing football, or board games, or reading the same book ten times in a row, or getting cross. I know you might have been hoping they'd go out and kick a ball around with the kids so you could get on with something else, but your parents have paid their dues, and they're your kids. Get over it.

You need to let your parents and in-laws do it their way, if only because you have no choice. But remember, your kids probably have more than one grandparent (I know some with up to eight, where both original sets split up and then found new partners) so the chances are that they have at least one grandparent who is happy to play football or read repetitively. Each grandparent will have their own strengths and weaknesses, and that's fine from your children's perspective.

You may have to work on your weak spots as a parent and try to be all things, but grandparents have been there, done that, and now they're free to play to their strengths and just avoid their weaknesses altogether.

I know this can be frustrating, but that's your stuff. Just focus on the positive things they will do, not the irritation of the things they won't. And be grateful that they're there at all.

And remember, when you finally have grandchildren of your own, it will be your turn to cherry-pick the activities you want to get involved in. When that time comes, you'll most likely look back and think, 'Oh OK. Now I get it'.

> # FOCUS ON THE POSITIVE THINGS THEY WILL DO, NOT THE IRRITATION OF THE THINGS THEY WON'T

RULE 3

Don't ask too much of them

Let's face it, it's exhausting being a parent. Whether your child is 6 months, 6 years or 16. Not only is it exhausting, but it can be pretty complicated logistically, and more so with every child you have. Fitting childcare round work, doing the school run, taking your kids to sports training or picking them up from friends' houses, organizing birthday parties, letting the hems down on all those clothes they keep outgrowing.

What you really need is help, and plenty of it. And look, there's your mum or dad, full of experience and just the perfect candidate to muck in and make your life a bit easier.

Hold up there a minute. Your parents have done this once already – when they were younger and had more energy – and you can't assume they want to do it again. Most grandparents want to get involved, but they have a limit. You need to make sure you don't ask them to overstep that. Don't wait for them to say no; don't ask unless you're sure they're willing.

Whether your parents work or not, live near or far, are together or single or with a new partner, are 40 or 80, seem busy or look as if they have lots of time on their hands, this is *your* child, and they don't owe you any time at all. They put in all their graft years ago, and they're entitled to time off now. Maybe the reason they look as if they have lots of free time is because that's how they like it, and they've earned it.

Of course, if they want to help out that's great, and most grandparents will want to help to some extent. But however much help they offer, always remember:

- They don't have the energy they used to have.
- They have other things they want to fit into their lives now.

- It's harder work looking after other people's children than your own, even when they're your grandchildren – your parents are constrained by your rules.

- Be grateful. Every time.

- Just because they're doing it now, doesn't mean you can assume they'll do it next time you ask. They're allowed to say no and you will accept it graciously when they do.

So establish with your parents what does and doesn't work for them. Maybe they're happy to help out during the day but like to keep their evenings free, or their weekends. Maybe they'll give the children lifts but aren't up for cooking meals for them. Maybe they don't mind looking after the kids overnight but prefer to do it in their own house.

Keep an eye on what you ask of your parents and in-laws, especially as the children grow and the kind of help you need changes. Make sure they're getting plenty of space and downtime, as well as getting to spend time with their grandchildren.

> ## MOST GRANDPARENTS WANT TO GET INVOLVED, BUT THEY HAVE A LIMIT

RULE 4

Don't guilt-trip them – even by mistake

So we're agreed that you need to look out for your parents' needs and to be appreciative of everything they do for you. But it gets trickier. Let me tell you about a friend of mine who is a grandparent. He picks the children up from school every day because his daughter works, and he takes them home and gives them something to eat before she gets back. She's a single parent, and occasionally she needs to go away overnight for work, so he stays and looks after the kids, and gets them up and off to school in the morning.

Here's what he told me a few months ago: 'I love the grandkids to pieces, and it's great spending time with them. But as I get older I'm finding it more and more exhausting. The trouble is, my daughter couldn't do the job if I didn't help out. She depends on me, so I can't say anything, but I wish I could have a day off sometimes.'

And there's the problem. If your parents think that you can't manage without them, that's a really unfair pressure to put on someone who is already doing you a favour. Yes, I know that sounds tough, but it's true. Let them know how grateful you are, but don't ever let them feel trapped. Tricky balancing act, but if you're going to ask them for help, you need to learn to do it.

My friend may be right that his daughter couldn't do her job without help. But actually she could pay a childminder once or twice a week, or find a friend to help out, or even find another job with different hours. However, she won't do any of those things as long as her dad keeps pushing himself because he feels he's in a trap he can't escape. It's sad because she has no idea how he feels, and would be mortified if she did.

You have to find a balance between being grateful and laying a burden on your parents. Avoid phrases like 'I don't know what I'd do without you', because although they seem appreciative, they put pressure on grandparents. To you it's just a phrase, but if you say it you need to follow it up by saying it's not true and you'd find a way, just so they know they have a get-out clause.

Be vigilant for signs that your parents are starting to find the help they give you too much of a burden. And remember that things can change, and help they were happy to give before doesn't fit round their life so smoothly any more. Your mum might need to cut down on the help she gives you after her hip replacement. Now your father-in-law has met a new partner, he's reluctant to give up so many of his evenings. All of which is absolutely fine, because however routine and longstanding their involvement with your kids is, it's always a favour which you should never take for granted.

> # LET THEM KNOW HOW GRATEFUL YOU ARE, BUT DON'T EVER LET THEM FEEL TRAPPED

RULE 5

Learn to share

Here's a problem I can best illustrate with the example of someone I know. She was struggling to cope with three little ones and a partner who was away for work several days a week. She was managing because her parents-in-law helped out a lot. Even though they lived some way away, they would come down for a couple of days at a time about once a fortnight, and it gave her the breathing space she needed to keep on top of everything.

And then her husband's sister got pregnant. Not long before the baby was born, this sister's relationship split up. So the sister was left coping alone with a newborn baby, and the trauma of splitting up. What did the in-laws do? Well, what would you do in that situation? It's a tricky one, whichever way you look at it. The in-laws felt their daughter needed them most and, as she lived in the other direction, they started spending a lot of time with her. Of course they visited their other grandchildren when they could, but their visits were suddenly cut right back, along with the help they brought.

When other grandchildren come along there's almost always going to be some kind of reallocation of resources from the grandparents. What else can they do? But however logical it is, it can be very tough to cope with when you're relying on them for help. If you're the first to produce grandchildren it can be especially disruptive, although if you're the last it's worth sparing a thought for your siblings if they're going to lose out. Grandparents have only so much time they can give, and it's theirs to allocate as they choose – no one else has any rights in it.

Your nieces and nephews aren't the only reason you might have to start sharing your parents. If they're single, they might meet a new partner, if they have a parent still alive (your grandparent), they may need to start caring for them more. Or they may simply change jobs or get involved in some other activity that takes them away from you and your children.

Whether you need help from your parents, or simply value the relationship they have with your kids, this is especially tough to cope with if you just look at it from your own point of view. It's easy to be resentful, not only towards your parents but perhaps towards your brother or sister who has taken their attention away from you – oh yes, those old sibling rivalries can surface long after you feel you should have outgrown them. It's OK, that's normal. But now you're an adult you need to deal with this in an adult fashion. Look at it from your parents' viewpoint. Or imagine yourself 25 years on having to make the same choices when it comes to your own children. And, just as your mum and dad told you all those years ago, learn to share nicely.

> # WHEN OTHER GRANDCHILDREN COME ALONG THERE'S ALMOST ALWAYS SOME KIND OF REALLOCATION OF RESOURCES

They're new to this too

We go through childhood assuming that our parents know what they're doing. After all, being a parent is what they do, so obviously they must be competent at it. It's only when you become a parent yourself that you discover that most of us are making it up as we go along. At least with the first child. And just when you think you might be getting the hang of it, they enter a new age. Baby, toddler, pre-schooler, infant, junior, teenager – at each stage you're still a novice because you've never had a child that age before.

So, for your parents, when their children have children of their own it's a double whammy as they enter a whole new phase as a parent *and* simultaneously enter completely unchartered territory as a new grandparent. Yep, that's right, once again they're making it up as they go along.

But this time it's almost more difficult, as they most likely want to enjoy being a grandparent to the young one, at the same time as they are being a good parent to you. So if you find yourself getting frustrated with Gran because she made an observation you didn't like, or feeling disgruntled with Granddad because you didn't like his reaction to your screaming toddler, try and bite it back. They've never done this before either you know.

There are lots of different ways to be a grandparent and, just like being a parent, not all of it is as instinctive as you'd like it to be. Your parents are finding their feet every step of the way, making it all up, and they have to do it in a way that works for them.

When your first child is born it's not easy to look up from the worries, nappies, lack of sleep and all the rest of it and pay attention to how your parents are coping. You're bound to leave them to get on with the grandparenting thing by themselves. By the time you look up, several months or even years later, they'll have established some kind of approach that they think seems to work. If, now you come to think of it, it's not an approach you like much, don't be hard on them. How were they to know? They had to make it up on the hoof if you remember.

What's more – and just to add to the fun – being a grandparent to a baby or a toddler is very different from being a grandparent to a 10-year-old, or a teenager. Same as with being a parent. So your parents and in-laws are having to adjust not only to their grandchildren's different personalities, but also to their different ages and stages.

Some grandparents take to their new role like a duck to water when your baby is born. But fast forward a dozen years and they may flounder when it comes to relating to a teenager two generations down from them.

So what's the Rule for you here? Well, if you have problems with the way your parents and in-laws behave as grandparents, of course you can broach them. But you need to do it very gently – people are understandably touchy about being criticized as a grandparent – and to recognize that it doesn't come instinctively, and you can't learn it from a book, or a YouTube video. So lower your expectations and cut them some slack. It's only fair, and if you feel more tolerant you're likely to stress less about their shortcomings.

LOWER YOUR EXPECTATIONS AND CUT THEM SOME SLACK

Understand that they don't come from the same place as you

Do you ever think about how different your children's lives are from your own? I do. I look back on a childhood without computers, mobile phones, umpteen TV channels. We spent half our lives out of doors (at least in memory). Teachers were allowed to tell us exactly what they thought of us, and parents would smack us if we misbehaved. It was a world apart. *And* a Mars bar only cost sixpence.

Now look further, back into the dim past that was your parents' childhood. They probably had to darn their own socks, walk everywhere and risk getting caned at school if they forgot their homework. Alright, maybe your parents weren't born as long ago as mine, but you get the point.

Styles of parenting have changed too. My parents' generation expected us to contribute more to the running of the house than most of today's parents, they certainly thought it was good sense to smack a naughty child, and they rarely discussed things with us – they just told us how it was.

Your own style as a parent is largely informed by your own experiences, the things you loved – and hated – as a child. You want to replicate certain idyllic bits of your childhood for your own kids, and avoid the harsh ones at all costs. I have one friend who would never make her children share a bedroom because she so hated having to share with her sister. And another who hated being alone and so makes sure that both his children sleep in the same room.

Your parents and in-laws have their own experiences, which are very different from yours. They may have had a strict upbringing which they feel worked for them, so that comes out in their style as a parent and grandparent. Or they may think that children should spend lots of time outdoors, or just eat what they're given and not make a fuss. You'll know roughly what your own parents' approach is, whether or not you think they were right. Your in-laws' attitude might be a long way from your comfort zone.

You'll have had some experience of this in all probability with your partner, who may not always see things the same way as you. However, as an equal shareholder, as it were, in the children it's easier to be understanding and try to find a compromise.

You don't *have* to compromise at all with your parents and in-laws. You could just tell them to butt out. However, if they're giving you their opinion it's because they care, and they believe their way is right. And actually, sometimes they might be right. So recognize that they have a different perspective from you, and learn to value their advice without necessarily accepting it. Every generation has a mix of ideas that have passed their sell-by date, and ideas that deserve to last. If you understand where the older generation is coming from, it's easier to pick out which is which.

LEARN TO VALUE THEIR ADVICE WITHOUT NECESSARILY ACCEPTING IT

Any grandparent is better than no grandparent

Not every parent is going to fit your idea of the perfect grandparent. Maybe you feel they were damaging as a parent, maybe they live much too far away, maybe the relationship is difficult since you split up with their son/daughter. Perhaps the effort to make it work all seems just too much.

Well, think again. Your child only has a finite number of grandparents. If you give up on the relationship on your child's behalf, you're denying them a bond they can't find elsewhere. Yes I know they can form strong friendships with other people of their grandparents' generation – I'm all for that, and it's great to see it, whether or not they are close to their grandparents. But it's not the same thing as a family link with someone who knows what your own parents were like as children, who can give you a sense of family history, who will love you unconditionally.

Some of my own children's relationships with my mother were in many ways much better than mine. I had my reservations about her as a parent, but she was a far better grandparent than I'd expected. I'm glad she had the chance to prove herself. It would have been easy for me to write her off and not bother to keep her in touch with the kids properly. But she made an effort and she genuinely cared for them, and they knew it.

So it's your job to fight on your child's behalf for them to have the best relationship they can with all their grandparents, at least until they're old enough to make their own decisions about who to have in their life. However much effort it takes, or swallowing of pride, just remember it's not about you. You're doing it for them.

You don't have to have the grandparents to lunch every weekend if you can't get along with them yourself. You can find a manageable way to organize things where you're not necessarily around, or the contact is in short bursts, or a few long stretches if distance is the problem. Come on, you can be creative about how to maximize the benefits for your child while minimizing the discomfort or difficulty for yourself.

I do recognize that there are a few genuinely abusive parents in the world who are best kept away from their grandchildren, but they are fortunately rare. Grandparents who simply have a different attitude or outlook or approach are fine – children are surprisingly flexible, in much the same way that they understand that rules at home and at school are different. And you're there to keep an eye of course. Parents who live at a distance are worth making the effort for. And parents or in-laws who you personally struggle to get along with can make grandparents who your child will love and appreciate. And when your child develops that special bond because of the hard work you put in to make it happen, it will be thanks to you.

> ## HOWEVER MUCH EFFORT IT TAKES, OR SWALLOWING OF PRIDE, JUST REMEMBER IT'S NOT ABOUT YOU

Don't bad-mouth them in front of the kids

Don't your parents drive you mad at times? And how about the in-laws? Very few of us have perfect relationships with the older generation, and some of us have decidedly sticky ones. Even when you broadly get on well, they're bound to have at least a few irritating habits, and possibly a wealth of infuriating ones. When you finally close the door after they leave, you may well find that sometimes you breathe a huge sigh of relief.

So how do you cope? Well, most of us release some tension by having a good moan to someone. That's human nature, and it's fine, but on no account should that someone be your child. Or anyone in earshot of them. It's not their job to help you dump the stress, so go and find someone else.

Why? Because it's impossible for your child to have a good relationship with their gran or granddad if they feel that you – whose judgement they instinctively trust – don't see them the same way. It's confusing and upsetting for them to see you feeling negatively towards someone they may feel positive towards. Their relationship with their grandparent is theirs to work out, and you sticking your oar in makes it much harder for them to do that.

I know what you want to ask. What if your child has a moan about their grandparent first? You're not changing their view then, are you? Yes you are, because you're reinforcing it, and making it more negative than it needs to be. Besides, your child might have a bit of a moan now but have forgotten it by tomorrow. But they won't forget you agreeing with them about how Granddad never shuts up, or how ratty Gran can be.

What do you do then? I'll tell you what you do. You sympathize with your child if they've been upset, but you put the case for the defence. You point out kindly that Gran gets very tired and her arthritis is bad, so it's harder to be even-tempered. You remark that Granddad might talk a lot, but that's because he's interested and enthusiastic.

If you're bringing your child up even half-right, they'll be able to form their own opinion eventually. Until they do, you have to do everything in your power to nurture and support their relationships with their grandparents. Even if they can be deeply irritating.

THEIR RELATIONSHIP WITH THEIR GRANDPARENT IS THEIRS TO WORK OUT

They love you just like you love your kids

For most of us, when we're little our parents are the most important thing in the world. We can't imagine them not being there, and we feel we simply couldn't cope if they weren't. Our world revolves around them.

As we get older they are still central to our lives, but we spend more time away from them and their importance is less central. Then we start to get into long-term relationships, and our partner is even more important than our parents. Once we have children, they become the focus of our lives (along with our partner) so that our parents, much as we still love them, are no longer the focal point as they used to be. We've moved on.

But what has happened to our parents? Well, consider how you'll feel about your own kids in 20 years or so. Will you have moved on? I doubt it. However strong and enduring your relationship with your partner, your children's happiness will always be crucial to your own. They will always be among the most important people in the world to you.

Have you noticed how much parents – of any age – talk about their kids? When older friends meet each other they almost always ask after the children – or the parents volunteer the information without waiting to be asked. Of course we sometimes talk about our parents but it's not generally such a focus of conversation.

So while you've moved on from your parents, up to a point, to focus on your partner and your children, for them you are still central just as your children will be to you in years to come. In other words, they still love you as strongly and fiercely as you love your kids and they always will.

Listen, I'm not trying to guilt-trip you here about how much time you spend with your parents. This is the way things are meant to be, with the love, attention, care, passion always cascading down from one generation to the next. But it can only help to be mindful of how much you mean to your parents, how much it matters to them that the relationship between you is strong and positive. They understand that you need to focus on your children – they went through the same process with their parents when you came along – but it doesn't stop them loving you and worrying about you. If you can recognize that and make the occasional nod to it, it will make all the difference to their world.

CONSIDER HOW YOU'LL FEEL ABOUT YOUR OWN KIDS IN 20 YEARS OR SO

HAD
ENOUGH
YET…?

Hey, it's not all parenting, you know. If you're smart, you'll want to learn how the most successful people behave at whatever it is: life, money, work, relationships, kids. Luckily I've done the hard work for you – the years of observing, the distilling and sieving and summarizing what really makes a difference into handy little Rules.

I've always been anxious not to stretch the Rules principle too far, but following huge demand from readers, I have tackled those big important areas that affect us all. So in the pages to follow you'll find a 'one Rule' taster of each of the other Rules books:

Rules of Life
Rules of Work
Rules of Wealth
Rules of Management
Rules of Love

See what you think. And if you like them there are plenty more in each of the books.

You'll get older but not necessarily wiser

There is an assumption that as we get older we will get wiser; not true I'm afraid. The rule is we carry on being just as daft, still making plenty of mistakes. It's just that we make new ones, different ones. We do learn from experience and may not make the same mistakes again, but there is a whole new pickle jar of fresh ones just lying in wait for us to trip up and fall into. The secret is to accept this and not to beat yourself up when you do make new ones. The Rule really is: be kind to yourself when you do muck things up. Be forgiving and accept that it's all part of that growing older but no wiser routine.

Looking back, we can always see the mistakes we made, but we fail to see the ones looming up. Wisdom isn't about not making mistakes, but about learning to escape afterwards with our dignity and sanity intact.

When we are young, ageing seems to be something that happens to, well, old people. But it does happen to us all and we have no choice but to embrace it and roll with it. Whatever we do and whoever we are, the fact is we are going to get older. And this ageing process does seem to speed up as we get older.

You can look at it this way – the older you get, the more areas you've covered to make mistakes in. There will always be new areas of experience where we have no guidelines and where we'll handle things badly, overreact, get it wrong. And the more flexible we are, the more adventurous, the more life-embracing, then the more new avenues there will be to explore – and make mistakes in of course.

As long as we look back and see where we went wrong and resolve not to repeat such mistakes, there is little else we need to do. Remember that any Rules that apply to you also apply to everyone else around you. They are all getting older too. And not any wiser particularly. Once you accept this, you'll be more forgiving and kinder towards yourself and others.

Finally, yes, time does heal and things do get better as you get older. After all, the more mistakes you've made, the less likely that you'll come up with new ones. The best thing is that if you get a lot of your mistakes over and done with early on in life, there will be less to learn the hard way later on. And that's what youth is all about, a chance to make all the mistakes you can and get them out of the way.

WISDOM ISN'T ABOUT NOT MAKING MISTAKES BUT ABOUT LEARNING TO ESCAPE AFTERWARDS WITH OUR DIGNITY AND SANITY INTACT

Get your work noticed

It's all too easy for your work to get overlooked in the busy hurly burly of office life. You're slaving away and it can be hard to remember that you need to put in some effort to boost your individual status and personal kudos for your work. But it's important. You have to make your mark so you stand out and your promotional potential will be realized.

The best way to do this is to step outside the normal working routine. If you have to process so many widgets each day – and so does everyone else – then processing more won't do you that much good. But if you submit a report to your boss of how *everyone* could process more widgets then you'll get noticed. The unsolicited report is a brilliant way to stand out from the crowd. It shows you're thinking on your feet and using your initiative. But it mustn't be used too often. If you subject your boss to a barrage of unsolicited reports, you'll get noticed but in completely the wrong way. You have to stick to certain rules:

- Only submit a report occasionally.

- Make really sure that your report will actually work – that it will do good or provide benefits.

- Make sure your name is prominently displayed.

- Make sure the report will be seen not only by your boss, but by their boss as well.

- Remember it doesn't have to be a report – it can be an article in the company newsletter.

Of course, the very best way to get your work noticed is to be very, very good at your job. And the best way to be good at your job is to be totally dedicated to doing the job and ignoring all the rest. There is a vast amount of politics, gossip, gamesmanship, time wasting and socializing that goes on in the name of work. It isn't work. Keep your eye on the ball and you'll already be playing with a vast advantage over your colleagues. The Rules Player stays focused. Keep your mind on the task at hand – being very good at your job – and don't get distracted.

THE UNSOLICITED REPORT IS
A BRILLIANT WAY TO STAND
OUT FROM THE CROWD

Anybody can be wealthy – you just need to apply yourself

The lovely thing about money is that it really doesn't discriminate. It doesn't care what colour or race you are, what class you are, what your parents did, or even who you *think* you are. Each and every day starts with a clean slate so that no matter what you did yesterday, today begins anew and you have the same rights and opportunities as everyone else to take as much as you want. The only thing that can hold you back is yourself and your own money myths.

> **YOU HAVE THE SAME RIGHTS AND OPPORTUNITIES AS EVERYONE ELSE TO TAKE AS MUCH AS YOU WANT**

Of the wealth of the world each has as much as they take. What else could make sense? There is no way money can know who is handling it, what their qualifications are, what ambitions they have or what class they belong to. Money has no ears or eyes or senses. It is inert, inanimate, impassive. It hasn't a clue. It is there to be used and spent, saved and invested, fought over, seduced with and worked for. It has no discriminatory apparatus so it can't judge whether you are 'worthy' or not.

I have watched a lot of extremely wealthy people and the one thing they all have in common is that they have nothing in common – apart from all being Rules Players of course. The wealthy are a diverse band of people – the least likely can be loaded. They vary from the genteel to the uncouth, the savvy to the plain stupid, the deserving to the undeserving. But each and every one of them has stepped up and said, 'Yes please, I want some of that'. And the poor are the ones saying, 'No thank you, not for me, I am not worthy. I am not deserving enough. I couldn't. I mustn't. I shouldn't'.

That's what this book is about, challenging your perceptions of money and the wealthy. We all assume the poor are poor because of circumstances, their background, their upbringing, their nurture. But if you have the means to buy a book such as this and live in comparative security and comfort in the world then you too have the power to be wealthy. It may be hard. It may be tough but it is doable. And that is Rule 1 – anyone can be wealthy, you just need to apply yourself. All the other Rules are about that application.

Get them emotionally involved

You manage people. People who are paid to do a job. But if it is 'just a job' to them, you'll never get their best. If they come to work looking to clock in and clock off and do as little as they can get away with in between, then you're doomed to failure, my friend. On the other hand, if they come to work looking to enjoy themselves, looking to be stretched, challenged, inspired and to get involved, then you are in with a big chance of getting the very best out of them. Trouble is, the jump from drudge to super team is entirely down to you. It is you that has to inspire them, lead them, motivate them, challenge them, get them emotionally involved.

That's OK. You like a challenge yourself, don't you? The good news is that getting a team emotionally involved is easy. All you have to do is make them care about what they are doing. And that's easy too. You have to get them to see the relevance of what they are doing, how it makes an impact on people's lives, how they provide the needs of other human beings, how they can reach out and touch people by what they do at work. Get them convinced – because it is true of course – that what they do makes a difference, that it contributes to society in some way rather than just lines the owner's or shareholder's pockets, or ensures that the chief executive gets a big fat pay cheque.

And yes. I know it's easier to show how they contribute if you manage nurses rather than an advertising sales team, but if you think about it, then you can find value in any role and instil pride in those who do whatever job it is. Prove it? OK. Well, those who sell advertising space are helping other companies, some of which may be very small, reach their markets. They are alerting potential customers to things they may have wanted for a long time and may really need. They are keeping the newspaper or magazine afloat as it relies on ad sales income, and that magazine or newspaper delivers information and/or gives pleasure to the people who buy it (otherwise they wouldn't, would they?).

Get them to care because that's an easy thing to do. Look, this is a given. Everyone deep down wants to be valued and to be useful. The cynics will say this is nonsense, but it is true, deep down true. All you have to do is reach down far enough and you will find care, feeling, concern, responsibility and involvement. Drag all that stuff up and they'll follow you forever and not even realize why.

Oh, just make sure that you've convinced yourself first before you try this out on your team. Do you believe that what you do makes a positive difference? If you're not sure, reach down, deep down, and find a way of caring...

> # GET THEM CONVINCED – BECAUSE IT IS TRUE OF COURSE – THAT WHAT THEY DO MAKES A DIFFERENCE

Be yourself

Isn't it just so tempting to reinvent yourself when you meet somebody new who you really fancy? Or to try and be who you think they are looking for? You could become really sophisticated, or maybe strong and silent and mysterious. At least you could stop embarrassing yourself by making jokes at inappropriate moments, or being pathetic about coping with problems.

Actually, no you couldn't. At least, you might manage it for an evening or two, or even a month or two, but it's going to be tough keeping it up forever. And if you think this person is the one – you know, the one – then you might be spending the next half century or so with them. Just imagine, 50 years of pretending to be sophisticated, or suppressing your natural sense of humour.

That's not going to happen, is it? And would you really want a lifetime of lurking behind some sham personality you've created? Imagine how that would be, unable ever to let on that this wasn't really you at all, for fear of losing them. And suppose they find out in a few weeks' or months' or years' time, when you finally crack? They're not going to be very impressed, and nor would you be if it was them who turned out to have been acting out of character all along.

I'm not saying you shouldn't try to turn over the occasional new leaf; improve yourself a bit. We should all be doing that all the time, and not only in our love life. Sure, you can try to be a bit more organized, or less negative. Changing your behaviour is all fine and good. This Rule is about changing your basic personality. That won't work, and you'll tie yourself in knots trying to do it convincingly.

So be yourself. Might as well get it all out in the open now. And if that's not who they're looking for, at least you won't get in too deep before they find out. And you know what? Maybe they don't actually like sophisticated. Perhaps strong silent types don't do it for them. Maybe they'll love your upfront sense of humour. Perhaps they want to be with someone who needs a bit of looking after.

You see, if you fake it, you'll attract someone who belongs with a person that isn't you. And how will that help? Somewhere out there is someone who wants exactly the kind of person you are, complete with all the flaws and failings you come with. And I'll tell you something else – they won't even see them as flaws and failings. They'll see them as part of your unique charm. And they'll be right.

> # MIGHT AS WELL GET IT ALL OUT IN THE OPEN NOW

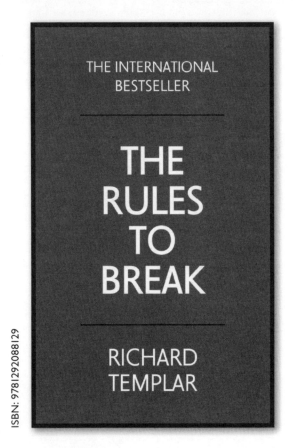